Happiness
is Success

Happiness *is* Success

By
AiR
Atman in Ravi

RUPA

Published by
Rupa Publications India Pvt. Ltd 2022
7/16, Ansari Road, Daryaganj
New Delhi 110002

Sales centres:
Allahabad Bengaluru Chennai
Hyderabad Jaipur Kathmandu
Kolkata Mumbai

Copyright © AiR Institute of Realization, 2022

All rights reserved.

No part of this publication may be reproduced, transmitted,
or stored in a retrieval system, in any form or by any means,
electronic, mechanical, photocopying, recording or otherwise,
without the prior permission of the publisher.

The views and opinions expressed in this book are the author's own and the facts
are as reported by him which have been verified to the extent possible,
and the publishers are not in any way liable for the same.

P-ISBN: 978-93-5520-192-8
E-ISBN: 978-93-5520-196-6

First impression 2022

10 9 8 7 6 5 4 3 2 1

The moral right of the author has been asserted.

Printed in India

This book is sold subject to the condition that it shall not, by way
of trade or otherwise, be lent, resold, hired out, or otherwise circulated,
without the publisher's prior consent, in any form of binding or
cover other than that in which it is published.

*I dedicate this book to my spiritual master,
Dada J.P. Vaswani*

CONTENTS

Preface ix

Part A: Success and Happiness
1. Why Does Everyone Want Success? 3
2. Is Success Happiness? 9
3. Achievement Is Only a Momentary Pleasure 13
4. The Paradox of Success 17
5. All Successful People Are Not Happy! 20
6. Can We Be Successful All the Time? 23
7. The Illusion of Success 28
8. Success Can Make Us Unhappy 32
9. The Race to Be an Ace Gets Us Caught in a Maze 36

Part B: The Happiness Journey
10. What Is True Happiness? 41
11. Do You Know What Makes You Happy? 45
12. Happiness Is a Choice 48
13. Flip Over from NEP to PEP 51
14. The Magic of Contentment and Fulfilment 55
15. Happiness Exists in the 'Now' 58
16. Mind: The Biggest Enemy of Happiness 62
17. Peace Is the Foundation of Bliss 66
18. Discover the Rainbow of 'True' Love 69

19. A Smile Doesn't Cost Anything	72
20. The Simple Secret to Happiness	75
21. Count Your Blessings and You Will Be Happy	78
22. Can We Be Happy All the Time?	81
23. The Pleasure–Pain Principle	85
24. Identify the Messengers of Misery	88
25. Triple Suffering Kills Our Happiness	92
26. Our Ignorance Makes Us Suffer	96
27. The Ultimate Secret of Everlasting Bliss, Joy and Peace	99
28. Happiness Is Like Your Shadow	104

Part C: Happiness Is Success

29. The Happiness Paradox	109
30. What Do People Assume Happiness to Be?	113
31. Happiness Is Not a Destination	118
32. Can We Control the Results of Our Actions?	121
33. The Art of Acceptance	124
34. Surrender Is the Way	127
35. Live Life Moment by Moment	130
36. Make Happiness a Habit	133
37. We Are Human Beings, Not Human Doings	136
38. In the End, We Will Have Success, But No Time	139
39. Live Before You Die	142
40. Success Is Not Happiness, Happiness Is Success	145
41. Choose to Be Happy, Not Successful	148

Afterword   152

PREFACE

All successful people are not happy,
But all happy people are successful.

—AiR

Isn't it strange that the whole world is seeking happiness, but to be happy we are chasing success? We live with the fallacy that if we are successful, we will be happy. We do not realize that it is the reverse that is true: success is not happiness, happiness is success!

Everybody wants to be an achiever, a winner. Nobody wants to be a loser. Why is the whole world caught in this race for success? What is the reward of success that makes people so passionate to win? If we go deep into the psychology of winning, we realize that people want to win because they believe that success will make them happy, just as failure will make them miserable. The very objective of being successful is to 'gain happiness'. Does anybody want success that will make them miserable? We are taught that if we are successful, we will be happy. We believe in this illusion and we live our life trying to climb the ever-changing peak of success, but we forget to be happy!

This is the paradox of success! People chase success and finally achieve their dreams, but they remain unhappy. Why? Because we, human beings, are never satisfied. Regardless of whatever we

HAPPINESS IS SUCCESS

achieve, we still want more. We want success because we believe that it will give us that much-needed home, our dream car or a much-awaited holiday, which we think will make us happy. But in the end, are we really happy? For the moment, yes! But soon, thereafter, we are thirsty for more. No doubt success creates a sense of instant gratification that makes us temporarily happy.

After over twenty-five years of intense search for success and happiness, I realized a simple but profound truth—I don't need to be successful to be happy. Staying happy is being successful. Why did it take me twenty-five years to come to this realization? Because, like everyone else, I wanted to be happy and so, I followed the herd by chasing success. One success after another, and one personal achievement after another, created excitement in my life. Every dream that was realized added a feather in my cap, and I thought I was gaining more and more happiness.

I had a store of about 2,000 square feet. I wanted more success, so I opened a 20,000-square-foot store. Though it was ten times bigger, my happiness was only marginally more. Instead, with all the success came stress, worry and anxiety, which took away most of the joy that success created.

Being human, I did not stop at that—I wanted to open a much bigger store. This time it was 2,00,000 square feet. I struggled and took many loans and spent over ten years realizing that dream until I finally realized something profound—I was achieving success, but what was I losing? I was losing out on life itself.

Thus, before I set out to achieve my next dream—this time it was to build a megacity with malls, hotels, golf courses, casinos, all innovatively designed on a space of about 200 acres of land—I thank my stars that I stopped. I said to myself, 'No! It's enough!' I did not want to exchange my life for success. Finally, I knew that I would have a lot of success and money in the bank, but I

PREFACE

would have no life left. I got off the success highway for good. This choice transformed my life. I shut down my business and decided to do things that I was passionate about, things that would make me truly happy.

I realized that happiness is not about personal achievements. Of course, success gave me money, name and fame, but these did not enhance my happiness quotient. For twenty-five years, it seemed like I had been blind to this reality. The only thing that mattered to me was success. I was passionate and rarely missed achieving a goal that I had set for myself. Instead of writing simple vision and mission statements that people talk of, I used to write much fiercer 'obsession statements'. As each year dissolved into the next, the money in my bank account kept increasing, just as the value of my property and my net worth kept going up. I am fortunate that I realized I was exchanging this for a resource that was limited—life itself! I knew that I would not live forever. One day, whatever I earn, somebody else will burn. I stopped. I changed. I transformed my life.

Instead of chasing success, I started doing HIS work—Humanitarian, Inspirational and Spiritual work. Instead of just making money, I was now making a difference, and this gave me true joy. Today, I live each day with joy, each moment with bliss. How did I reach this state of ananda or pure bliss? In my quest for happiness, I discovered several secrets to happiness, secrets that were actually not secrets but principles. Since they remained unknown to the world, I call them secrets. I have enjoyed the last ten years of my life in pure ecstasy by living with these principles.

As I left the highway of achievement, I found others speeding towards destination success. Like me, they too believed in the fallacy: success is happiness. However, success could never satisfy my needs because greed had taken charge of my life. Success has no ultimate destination as human beings are never satisfied. After one success, we want another and still another, so there is no destination called success. That's why some people realize that success is a journey, not a destination.

> *We can't be successful all the time*
> *but we can be blissful all the time.*

In this race for success, I am grateful that I finally realized what I truly wanted. It was happiness, but I was caught in the wrong chase, so I shut my shop. I realized that happiness from contentment was far more fulfilling than the pleasure derived from personal achievement. I switched over from seeking pleasure to living in peace, the very foundation of happiness.

I immersed myself in humanitarian work, and that gave me bliss. I began writing motivational books and giving transformational talks to instil positive energy in people. I spent time writing bhajans or life songs to help people become believers and live with faith, hope and enthusiasm. All this made my life blissful and peaceful. I was blessed when I stopped living a life that was just meant to chase success.

Today, as I look around, the world is gripped by fear of death and disease that has stolen our happiness. COVID-19 brought the entire world to a standstill from March 2020 till the end of 2021. Instead of living with precaution, we have let panic shape our actions and tried to use the *cannon to kill the mosquito* (Confucius). Our mind has, once again, stolen our peace, the very foundation of happiness. Every now and then, a pandemic, a tsunami, a volcano or a humanitarian crisis will envelop our lives. This should not steal our happiness. It is part and parcel of karma, the universal law that unfolds on earth. We must learn to accept, to surrender and to move on. Whatever is within our control, we must take

PREFACE

charge of it but we must not lose our smile, our bliss and our peace. If we learn to live with faith, trust, hope and enthusiasm, our happiness will be in place. After all, nothing is more important than to be happy.

This book will help you realize that in this journey of life, success, no doubt, leads you to several peaks, but it often brings you down to a valley of dissatisfaction and disappointment. Success is making the best of the moment and the only way to live joyously in each moment is to be happy in the 'now', to live each moment as it unfolds. This is true success and it is all about being happy.

I hope this book will help you master the art of happiness as you live your life with peace, the foundation of joy; with true love, the fountain of happiness; and without any misery that is inflicted upon us by none other than our own mind. Instead of chasing success to be happy, you should try to be happy. That is true success. Those reading this for the first time may think that this is just a tongue twister. It's not! It's a principle that humanity must learn. *Success is not happiness, happiness is success.*

PART A
....
SUCCESS AND HAPPINESS

Everybody wants to be happy, and so we seek success.
We may earn achievements, but our life will have stress.
Success, of course, makes us happy, but it is a momentary pleasure.
Happiness is not success. When will we find the real treasure?

Success creates name and fame; it also creates wealth.
Success will give us money, but it can't guarantee health.
Success makes us champions, whom the whole world will know,
but it won't give peace and bliss that will make our face glow.

—AiR

1
WHY DOES EVERYONE WANT SUCCESS?

The whole world is seeking success,
when all they want is bliss.
They land up with a lot of money in the bank,
but true happiness they miss.

—AiR

Who doesn't want to succeed? It seems like the whole world is chasing success. From the time we are conscious about who we are, the success journey starts. A child in school wants to come first in class. Teenagers have academic goals just as they also have dreams about relationships with the ones they love. As we grow older, we assume success to be all about achieving wealth, name and fame.

Different achievements are considered 'successes' by different people. To a politician, it may be winning an election. To a model, it is wearing the crown of a beauty pageant. To a sportsman, it may be becoming the world champion. Success is something entirely different to a millionaire. He now wants to be a billionaire. While different people pursue different things in life, each of us wants to be an achiever. Why is it that we are so passionate about success?

We seek success because it creates excitement and happiness? Who would want an achievement that would make him miserable. The objective of achievement is happiness. Therefore, the moment we embark on the journey of life, we develop aspirations that are meant to give us fulfilment. However, there are some people who are not passionate about success. Either they are just lazy, or they live in their comfort zone. Deep down in their heart, however, they too wish for success, but they don't want it as badly because they are not willing to pay the price to be a winner.

I started my success journey when I was just sixteen. I set up an unconventional advertising agency where I worked for a few hours after attending school. I got the first taste of success when I made enough money in two years to make a down payment to buy my own car. It was a moment of great joy! I had never experienced such ecstasy in the earlier eighteen years of my life. Those who succeed know how it feels when, for the first time, the world calls us an achiever. However, we human beings are strange. As soon as the excitement of our one success wears out, our mind jumps to dream about our next achievement.

As circumstances would have it, I was forced to move into my family business of retailing. My obsession to be a winner made me strike gold, and I became the most successful modern retailer in the country. I made millions. Whatever I touched seemed to turn to gold. From a small rented property of 2,000 square feet, I earned enough money and courage to buy a property of 20,000 square feet. I was just eighteen when I started and even before I was twenty-five, I felt like a successful millionaire. I was determined to succeed. Of course, success comes with a cost. I used to work eighteen hours a day, all days of the week, but I felt that I never worked at all! It was fun. I was enjoying my career because I was minting money. The money got me everything I ever wished for—clothes, cars and holidays to all the exotic destinations. Wow! I was happy!

I am not the only one who was caught in this mad race to be successful. No doubt everybody can't be a winner—though everybody wants to. The ones who have not yet tasted success crave it far more than those who have been winners. Somehow, from an external perspective, they believe that successful people are the happiest people and they want success too.

Therefore, everybody aspires to be a winner. Every golfer wants to be Tiger Woods. Every software engineer wants to be Bill Gates. But can every young man become successful like Charlie Chaplin? While everybody can't be successful, everybody wants to be. People believe that if they are successful, they will be blissful. Therefore, most of the world is willing to give up everything for success.

I have been riding on success for twenty-five years and not for a day did I stop. Those of us who succeed can't even sleep without dreaming about success. Not only do we take success to our dining tables, we often take it to our toilets, to the beach and wherever else we go. Such is success! It becomes an obsession. First, we chase success, but once it arrives, it chases us for the rest of our life.

There was once a man who used to envy his friends who owned warm, imported furry blankets. He always wished that he too could have such a blanket. This man used to live in the northern part of India where the river Ganges flows from the Himalayas. One day, as if it were a gift from the divine, he saw a beautiful rug floating down the river. Obsessed by the desire to possess his own rug, he immediately jumped into the water and started swimming. He swam until he could grab hold of the rug. His friends, who were watching from the banks of the river, started clapping, saying, 'Very good! But come back soon because the water starts to flow faster!' The man screamed back, 'It's not letting me go!' The friends were puzzled and wondered what was happening. Upon looking carefully, they realized that what they had all thought was a rug was actually not a rug, but a furry bear. Success is like that. First, we chase and grab it, and later, it catches hold of us and never lets go for the rest of our life.

I have spoken to many successful people and I found one thing in common. They are all busy achieving success and they say that 'one day' they will do what they love to do. Some of them are so intoxicated by their success journey that the pleasure they enjoy casts a shadow on true peace and bliss, which they unfortunately never experience.

When I turned forty, I stopped to contemplate. Was I truly happy with my monetary success and my business achievements? I am lucky that for the past decade of my life I have been doing things that I enjoy doing. These were not on the main menu of my success. They were my hobbies and my favourite pastimes. I started a humanitarian organization that picked people who were suffering on the streets and helped them recover so that we could put them back on their feet. I experienced a great sense of fulfilment in doing this and the few other things that I enjoyed doing. The joy I got from making a difference was far more rewarding than the pleasure I derived from making money. No doubt, buying my first Mercedes-Benz made me feel great, just as being chauffeur-driven in my limousine gave me a sense of achievement. Each pleasure, in fact, became the fuel to catapult me into my next endeavour. I became a slave to my success. There was no time to be truly happy! All my achievements that were meant to give me fulfilment were only creating excitement.

WHY DOES EVERYONE WANT SUCCESS?

While I looked around, all my peers had their focus on just one thing—success! I am a member of the Young Presidents' Organisation, an organization that enrols only successful leaders. I found that each member wanted to prove their success to the world. It seemed to me that the rich and famous lived each day of their life as if it was a 'success show', and they had to present their success to their peers and to the world to derive happiness. Were they truly happy? They were so enamoured by success that nothing else mattered.

What inspired me was that some people realized that life was not all about achieving success. There was something bigger than success. One such inspiration was Gurcharan Das. Just a year before I made my decision, I found him, then the CEO of Procter & Gamble India, taking early retirement to become a full-time writer. He was one such blessed soul who realized that success had a bigger meaning than just worldly achievement. Around the same time, Bill Gates announced that he would move out of Microsoft to devote his time to his foundation. To me, these were the people who truly understood the meaning of life. They did not shy away from stopping a journey that the world considered a success. They, too, took an exit from the highway of achievement to find more meaning in life.

I am grateful that I could see what lay ahead. I realized that I was not going to be alive forever. Every world champion must bow out one day. Every successful CEO has to make way for others. Can we be successful forever? I could see so clearly—the success the world is chasing is transitory. Still, out of ignorance, we seek nothing but success, whatever that success may mean to us.

I didn't want to be just another horse that was running because it had to reach the finish line. I stopped and asked myself questions like, 'Who am I? Why am I here? Is success actually making me happy? What is giving me more peace—is it the achievement of my success or my fulfilment that comes from doing the things I love?' With the help of my mentor, Dada J.P. Vaswani, I took a call. Dada was not just my mentor; he was my best friend too. One day, he said something that completely changed my life. 'Ravi, you are not meant for this world. You have a different purpose. What would you do with more wealth and possessions? Your heart belongs elsewhere, your soul is pure, and you are a lover of God. You seek God. You have my consent to shut down your business and move towards living a life of meaning and purpose.'

The world was shocked when a dynamic businessman, one who had set up India's largest departmental store, suddenly decided to shut it down in 2007. I was barely forty years old when I decided to move on from a life of making money to a life of making a difference.

My chase for success was over! The race to be an achiever had come to an end. I now wanted joy and bliss that would stem from peace. I started a new journey of life.

TAKEAWAYS

- The whole world is chasing success because we think that life is all about attaining personal achievement.
- The reason why people want success is that they think success or personal achievement is the source of their happiness.
- Most people get caught in the maze of success and before they realize it, their life is over!
- Very few people take an exit from the highway of success to pursue a life that gives them lasting peace and happiness.

2

IS SUCCESS HAPPINESS?

If success was happiness,
then the achievers would have a smile.
But look at them, many are lonely...
and their stress is longer than the Nile...

—AiR

Success is addictive. Once you achieve success, not only do you feel good about yourself, you start looking at your next victory. At first, the achievement gives a lot of pleasure. But soon, the happiness born out of success starts to decrease. If I look back at my life, I was far happier achieving smaller victories in my earlier days than the bigger championships of later life. Why didn't more success bring me more happiness?

If we look around at all the successful people in the world, can we see them enjoying eternal happiness? Unfortunately, no! Successful people enjoy all the pleasure that comes from making their dreams come true, but they get lost in the maze called success.

Therefore, success is not happiness. While it begins our journey of smiles and laughter, very soon, we get so lost in the process of

HAPPINESS IS SUCCESS

achievement that fulfilment takes a back seat. In the beginning, every winner enjoys happiness and dances with the joy of victory. Soon, the victory makes him continue the dance, but the joy disappears.

Why is it that success that initially brings so much happiness soon ceases to be a source of our bliss? Because success comes with a price to pay. Success doesn't come easily. If somebody who is not yet successful thinks that success is sheer luck, or it comes by chance, and the achievers of this world are just fortunate to be born as successful people, they are incorrect. Success consumes our life, so much that we are so focused on success that we forget that the goal of our success was happiness.

Once we are drugged with victory, the intoxication to succeed surpasses all our priorities, and we forget to live. We end up becoming machines producing success.

Success has indeed made me a wealthy man. My ego rose to the sky, and I felt superior. But now, I had to manage many more things. The most important was, 'What does the world think of me?' My attention went to what clothes I wore, how comfortable the guests were when they came to my home, which parties I had to attend and so many other things, all of which made me forget happiness. Success kept me looking good, but the smile on my face was plastic and the laughter came from my head rather than my heart. I became a puppet of this monster called success.

Every winner will admit that success carries with it stress and anxiety. My life too was full of stress, worry and fear. Why? Because success is such! It is stronger than any other addiction that the world sees. I rarely find a person who becomes a world champion and sits down to enjoy the achievement. I haven't met a millionaire who said 'It's enough!' barring a few lucky ones who broke the addiction of success to live a fulfilling life. Kudos to people like Bill Gates and Gurcharan Das. They are the real monks who sold their

IS SUCCESS HAPPINESS?

Ferraris. Most successful people get caught in the cycle of success. To them, they have no choice, they must keep on pedalling; if they stop, they will fall! And so, the focus of life is to move towards the next destination, rather than enjoying the journey.

I learned the truth behind this popular quote: 'Happiness is the journey itself, not the destination.' Success, unfortunately, makes us blind to the journey, because we are focused on the destination. Well, that is what success is all about—it is an accomplishment of a goal, making a dream come true. Success, as understood by the world, is not what 'true' success is. True success is understanding who we truly are and what the purpose of our life on earth is. But this is not what the world understands success to be. To the world, success is money, it is being on the cover of *Time* magazine. It is being covered by the *BBC* or *CNN*. People measure success by the amount of money they have in the bank, their assets and their rewards. When this becomes the success that we seek, happiness disappears like mist in the morning sun.

Of course, it feels good to be rich and famous, to have financial security; but is that happiness? The happiness that comes from making money is minuscule when compared to the happiness that comes from sharing it. Most people are doing otherwise. When the millionaires of the world spend their money, it is more for the sake of maintaining their image. Therefore, in today's world, luxury brands continue to be appreciated because they become an outlet for the wealthy to show off their success. We begin to believe that all this wealth and show will lead us to the destination of happiness, but this is like a mirage in the desert. It doesn't exist!

An acquaintance of mine was once sharing his life story. For forty years, he had achieved success after success. He grew from a millionaire to a billionaire and lived in Hong Kong in a luxurious villa. But the rich man was now suffering from the final stages of cancer, and this is what he said: 'If only I had spent my life sharing my wealth, rather than just making it, I would have died a happier man.'

TAKEAWAYS

- Success is achievement, name and fame.
- Success, unfortunately, is an addiction. We get so intoxicated with success that happiness takes a back seat.
- Success takes away our peace, which is the key to happiness.
- We believe that all this wealth will lead us to the destination of happiness, but it never happens because 'Happiness is the journey itself, not the destination'.

3

ACHIEVEMENT IS ONLY A MOMENTARY PLEASURE

Of course, achievement will surely give us pleasure,
But lost in success, we forget the real treasure.

—AiR

For those who think that success is happiness, this is news. Success gives us happiness for the moment, but soon, that happiness dissolves into the journey of success itself.

Success is about achievement. Different people have different aspirations, and define success in different ways. But, by and large, success is considered to be an achievement in the material world. In the spiritual world, the word 'success' doesn't find a place to survive. Therefore, success, or the achievement of a dream or a goal, has more to do with money, name, fame, title or position.

It is important to clarify the various achievements that can come under the umbrella of 'success' before we *analyse* whether success and achievement can lead to true happiness. Achievements in the world can be broadly classified into business achievements,

achievements in the world of sport and art, achievements in politics and even achievements in the field of religion or education. There may be many other streams of achievement that fall under these broad categories as the world has grown into a sphere of super-specializations. But ultimately, those who want to be achievers are seeking one of these primary objectives. People don't want to succeed for nothing! They want money or fame. Some may only want success for personal satisfaction, but still, that persistent desire to succeed creates wheels under their feet that make them roll through life towards the destination they seek.

Having understood what success is to the world, the picture becomes clear. It leads only to pleasure, which is momentary. Achievement does not give us contentment. Just like gamblers are addicted and they will keep on hoping for a bigger bounty from the casino, achievers, too, keep on investing their life for the next achievement. Though there is a big difference: the gambler only has money to lose at the casino while the achievers end up losing something more profound—life itself! The achiever enjoys the moment of ecstasy that comes with the achievement but is so caught up in reaching the peak of success that his life is consumed and is soon over. Mark Cuban, a self-made billionaire, once said, 'Don't follow your passion. Those passions aren't worth a nickel!' According to Cuban, time is our most valuable asset and how we use it is most important, more important than just running behind our passion.

While every achiever wants to be happy, there is only one thing that is greater than this desire to be happy—to take their achievement further. This desire to go on and on in the journey called success stops achievers from enjoying the journey called life.

My life, too, was a life of achievements. Every achievement gave me great pleasure. I kept aside the rewards of success so that

ACHIEVEMENT IS ONLY A MOMENTARY PLEASURE

I could enjoy them a little later. I had to pay attention to my next dream. My first store consumed me round the clock and gave me well-deserved rewards. But it also gave me a dream to open the biggest kids' clothing store in the country. I spent the next five years travelling to many successful malls in the world and created amazing success. As Kids Kemp grew into Big Kids Kemp, a store ten times bigger, there was more money in the bank and I was covered by many newspapers and magazines and several television channels. Who doesn't enjoy being a celebrity? Everything was great, except that I had no time. Time was consumed pursuing success and achievement. The property that housed this project was purchased through a loan from the bank, and I had to pay it back in instalments. I thank God that I was able to pay back the loan in half the duration because the project was a great success.

This led me to my next achievement, to open a store that was 200,000 square feet, again, ten times bigger than the previous one. I spent years completing this project. The property was ten times the value of the previous property. The world thought I was the most successful innovative retailer they knew, and they were applauding my success journey, which by then had seen about twenty years of non-stop success. The story of my achievement went on, but soon I realized how momentary happiness is when it is born out of achievement. It is just like eating your favourite pizza or watching a good movie. This is just pleasure. It comes and it goes. People confuse this with happiness.

Why is it that achievement cannot give the lasting happiness that bliss is all about? This is because human beings are basically greedy. We want more and more. We are not able to stop after an achievement and then pursue a life of contentment and fulfilment. We put this off for a future date, which unfortunately never comes. No doubt, the achievers are not unhappy in their work. Their achievement gives them great excitement, but it doesn't give them true happiness. They don't even know the meaning of happiness because they are so busy succeeding and enjoying the momentary pleasure of each success. It is only much later, when life makes us introspect on our true purpose, that we realize that achievement actually robbed our life away from us. In the guise of giving us pleasure, achievement stole our peace, the very foundation of happiness.

TAKEAWAYS

- Our achievement gives pleasure, but the pleasure doesn't last.
- Achievement seems to be a peak every winner tries to climb. But, in reality, there is no peak. This is a mirage, an illusion.
- Happiness from success is a temporary pleasure. We go from need to greed. Attaining personal achievements stops us from being contented and fulfilled.
- The pleasure derived from our achievement robs us of peace, which is the very foundation of happiness.

4
THE PARADOX OF SUCCESS

Maybe that's enlightenment enough: to know that there is no final resting place of the mind, no moment of smug clarity. Perhaps wisdom… is realizing how small I am, and unwise and how far I have yet to go.

—Anthony Bourdain

Celebrity chef Anthony Bourdain ended his life. Hollywood A-lister Robin Williams committed suicide because of depression. People often wonder why people who succeed, who become world champions, who attain a high position in politics, who make millions, who top their class, who become rich and famous or even accumulate awards and accolades, remain unsatisfied? This is the paradox of success, which has now become a subject of discussion worldwide.

This paradox reveals that success and achievement will make us happy, but we soon realize that success is not a direct means to happiness. It may make us enjoy pleasure momentarily, but if success was happiness, then more success should have delivered more happiness. Then the rich and the famous, the millionaires and the billionaires would be the happiest people in the world! A few years later, in Bengaluru, V.G. Siddhartha, the founder of India's first coffee chain, ended his life by jumping into a river. Why did a millionaire commit suicide? The objective of pursuing success is happiness. But if success leads to stress and anxiety to such an extent that one commits suicide, then that is not success.

What is the cause of this paradox of success? It is greed. John was desperate to become a millionaire. He worked very hard and finally made it to the millionaires' club. He was happy, but he was not satisfied. He wanted to make his second million, his fifth and even his tenth million. Although he was successful, he had no contentment. John is not the only one caught in this paradox of success. Most of humanity, by nature, is never satisfied. Though they achieve much-desired success, they only pause momentarily to jump into the next desire. Soon, the joy from the reward of success starts diminishing and then, making a million, for instance, is no longer exciting.

When we are always comparing our success with that of others instead of becoming happy with our own, we become unhappy. When we are not successful, we get disappointed and dejected and the very pursuit of success, which was meant to give us joy, makes us miserable. Much is said about that girl who cried because she did not win the crown in the beauty pageant. She got the second position. While she was in tears, the girl who came third was jumping in excitement because she had not expected to win at all.

The paradox of success, therefore, makes us realize that success is not success. It makes us realize that achievement can never give us fulfilment. Many of the most successful people in the world have come out in the open and admitted that they are depressed although they are successful. Bollywood superstar Deepika Padukone has come out in the open about her struggle with depression. If somebody is as successful as Deepika, why then would she call every second of life a struggle? Isn't this a paradox?

For those who believe that success is happiness, it remains a paradox. They can't digest the fact that successful people can be miserable. However, those who are enlightened with the truth and who realize that success is not happiness aren't surprised by the state of such successful people. Their jaws don't drop when they hear of successful people living a miserable life. Success is only achievement. It doesn't guarantee happiness. That's why all successful people in this world are not necessarily truly happy people.

TAKEAWAYS

- Successful people who have everything, experience stress, anxiety and even depression, which only reveals the paradox of success.
- Instead of being content, successful people compare their success with others and become unhappy.
- Success is success. It doesn't guarantee happiness.
- If success leads to stress and anxiety to such an extent that one commits suicide, then that is not success.

5

ALL SUCCESSFUL PEOPLE ARE NOT HAPPY!

To give someone a piece of your heart is worth more than all the wealth in the world.

—Michael Jackson

What does success do? It creates so much baggage that our life ends in a mess. Success creates stress. We are constantly worried, both about our successes and our failures. Either way, we lose our peace of mind. To add to it, success creates fear because of the expectation that success carries with it. We worry so much about our dreams and our goals; where is the question of being happy? And if happiness comes, it only comes for that moment when we come face to face with our victory and then once again, the battle continues. Despite being successful, we are still discontented because our mind makes us ponder over our achievements. It makes us compare our success with that of others and we become jealous and lose our mental peace. All these are routine emotions in the life of winners. It is a price to pay for victory.

ALL SUCCESSFUL PEOPLE ARE NOT HAPPY!

Some successful people know how to manage their success. But the numbers are very few. Rare are those who put a full stop to their achievements after noteworthy success. They pause to live and enjoy their success. The others, most of the success clan, believe that success means succeeding again and again. How can you stop? The moment you stop climbing the success peak, you are a failure. Fear of failure ruins the happiness of most successful people.

I shocked many people when, suddenly, in 2007, I announced the shutting down of my business. To many of my peers it may have looked like a failure, but for me, it was the most successful moment of the first four decades of my life. I was finally free to live the life of my dreams. I was free from stress, worry and anxiety that go hand in hand with success. For the first time, I felt that it was so strange that people were pursuing success for happiness. Success, to me, seemed to be something that destroys happiness. But at that point, I was even scared to whisper this realization because the whole world believed that success would lead to happiness.

Howard Hughes, the well-known business tycoon, aviator and filmmaker, produced and directed many films, and dated many leading actresses of his time. He acquired enormous wealth and fame from his various ventures. He broke several aviation landmarks, designing airplanes himself, flying them and setting speed records. In the last twenty years of his life, he cut himself off from the outside world and went into complete seclusion, becoming his own prisoner. He died a lonely man.

Marilyn Monroe, one of the twentieth century's biggest Hollywood stars, had a sad and disturbing private life and had difficulties coping with her fame. She divorced three times, never finding true happiness. Her final years were filled with sickness and personal problems, and she died under mysterious circumstances at the age of thirty-six.

HAPPINESS IS SUCCESS

Michael Jackson is said to have battled various demons throughout his life. Despite his astounding fortune, fame and popularity, he was often thought to be a sad and lonely superstar. Although he still had his life ahead of him, he died at the age of fifty due to cardiac arrest caused by acute intoxication of prescription drugs, on which he had become dependent.

These so-called successful people not only became unsuccessful, but also felt unhappy and miserable so much so that some of them even died by suicide—then why does the world believe that success is happiness? Isn't it enough proof that success is neither directly related nor directly proportional to happiness?

TAKEAWAYS

- People pursue success because they think success is happiness.
- Success creates so much baggage that our life ends in a mess. Success creates stress and we are constantly worried, both about our successes and our failures.
- If success was happiness, then all successful people should be happy.
- If we look around, we will find the world is filled with successful people who are unhappy and lead a miserable life.

6
CAN WE BE SUCCESSFUL ALL THE TIME?

The whole world is chasing success,
everyone wants achievement.
Sometimes we win, sometimes we lose,
there is no contentment.

—AiR

When I analysed success and tried to understand why success doesn't create happiness, I realized that there is a simple truth that we fail to take into account. By itself, success is all about success, not about failure. Winners believe that they must win all the time. To them winning is not the main thing; it is 'the only' thing. If a world champion in chess loses a chess tournament, his ego is devastated. He was once the world champion! How could he lose? To him, there was nobody else who could do better in chess. He was the 'God' of chess! Haven't we seen this happen so often? The very success that promised bundles of joy becomes the cause of misery and sorrow.

Have you ever wondered what happens to a person who loses the presidential elections? All attention goes to the president and the oath-taking, and the media shuts its doors to the loser. But then, everybody cannot be president. We know it, but while we know how to accept success, we have not learned how to accept failure. It is not always competitive, where somebody has to win and somebody has to lose. For instance, sometimes when a batsman is on the cricket field, his fans expect him to score a century, but they don't realize that you can't hit a century in every match. When the champion is out on a low score, he is booed and jeered. It is strange that it's not just a single person who wins or loses. There's this myth that champions must always be champions. However, we don't realize that we can't be winners forever. There will be times when even the most successful people fail.

Man has been created in such a way that he ages, and over time, he becomes frail. Man cannot be in his prime forever. There are times when people go to a surgeon and treat him like a 'God'. They consider him to be a magician who can give life. For decades, the surgeon is successful, but one day, he gets a stroke. He is unable to perform surgery. Then what happens to him? Overnight, he loses everything. He is unable to digest the fact that his success journey has come to an end.

Most successful people, unfortunately, end their life as failures. Not so much because they fail in the real sense, but they fail to accept a natural decline that every human being must gracefully undergo. In the film industry, there are actors who performed at their peak, but with time, their era comes to an end. Is it a failure? Of course not! But those who don't understand that success is a phase, think of it as a failure. They experience withdrawal symptoms as they fade into the background as young and more enthusiastic people take over the stage. This is a law of the universe and we cannot escape it. Why then should we believe that we have to be successful all the time? When will the world realize the true meaning of success? Just like every rose has a thorn, success will be followed by failure before the end of our life.

We don't realize that winners can't win all the time. Even the most successful person fails one day. But success doesn't leave room for failure. It is this irony that causes us to become miserable. There are several keys that open the door to success. One such key is desire. Desire is the starting point of all achievements. It is also the key to failure. Every desire cannot be fulfilled. We may desire a hundred things and fulfil all our desires, but there will definitely be a day when our desire is not fulfilled. Then what happens? We become disappointed and disgruntled. We are unable to accept defeat. Isn't it strange that even though our desire was fulfilled a hundred times, the one unfulfilled desire can wipe out our entire treasure of happiness? Failures are like milestones on the highway of success, so we must learn to accept them. When Thomas Edison was young, his teachers told him that he was 'too stupid to learn anything'. In his own words, Edison said, 'I have not failed.' Although he failed a thousand times in the invention of the light bulb, he said, 'Great success is built on failure.'

Therefore, we are bound to become unhappy in our journey of success. I too experienced failure in my climb to the top. I know how it feels, just like every winner does. The fear of failure itself makes us lead a life of stress and anxiety. We are constantly worrying about the result of our efforts even though the results are not in our hands. As a competent achiever, there were times when I tried my best, but I failed. I could neither explain nor accept failure. I was successful. To me, as it does to any other successful person, success meant success, not failure. I would do anything and everything possible, by fair or foul means, to try to win, but I learned that it is just not possible to live a life of success without failing.

When successful people don't understand that they can't win all the time, and they don't learn to accept failure gracefully, they very often fall into depression. They either withdraw from the world, unable to show their face with the scars of defeat, or they take the ultimate step of ending their life. Isn't it really sad that something as beautiful as success, something as exciting as achievement, should end in such an unfortunate way? Why can't humanity accept success as it should be? Why can't we learn that nobody can be successful all the time. And, just as we celebrate our victories, why can't we learn to accept failure with humility and hold our head high?

It is because of our ignorance. Because we think that success means succeeding every time, we keep pushing ourselves. Our ignorance makes us suffer when we miss the mark. Our ignorance is based on the belief that success is happiness. We need to change our attitude. Just as we laugh when we are successful, we must learn to smile when we fail. We are so obsessed and passionate about success that we fail to learn this lesson and thus end our life in misery.

Of course, we want to be happy. Who doesn't? But success is not the only way to be happy. While it is good to be successful, we have to learn a way to be peaceful and not live our life filled with stress and anxiety. If we believe the false notion that success is happiness, and spend our entire life chasing success, we can achieve a lot of success, but end up with our life in a mess. When will we realize the truth?

CAN WE BE SUCCESSFUL ALL THE TIME?

TAKEAWAYS

- Although success is not something permanent, we do not accept the fact that we can't be successful all the time.
- Because we do not understand that we cannot be successful all the time, we become miserable; some of us retreat from our successful life, withdrawing from the world with frustration and embarrassment, and some even die by suicide.
- It is because of our ignorance that we think that success means succeeding every time, and so we keep pushing ourselves.
- Just as we laugh when we are successful, we must learn to smile when we fail.

7
THE ILLUSION OF SUCCESS

The belief that success is happiness is an illusion.
We are seeking happiness, but there is some confusion.
Like the rainbow, which only seems to be in the sky,
we keep chasing the success illusion till we die.

—AiR

We all admire a rainbow in the sky. A rainbow appears when the light of the sun shines through droplets of rainwater; and the seven colours of the rainbow can be seen against the backdrop of the sky. But if we try to touch a rainbow, we can't! It is an illusion. It is like a mirage in the desert. Similarly, success appears to give us happiness. But the happiness that comes from success is only an illusion. It doesn't exist. Why is this so?

An achievement promises us pleasure, but the pleasure soon dissolves into stress, worry and anxiety. Thus, happiness appears for a moment, but soon disappears like a rainbow. In my journey of life, I spent twenty-five years trying to be happy with success. But even after a silver jubilee of consistent success, I couldn't find lasting happiness. There was so much commotion that there was no

THE ILLUSION OF SUCCESS

time to be still and enjoy peace. Today, when I watch a beautiful sunset, I reflect on how during the two and a half decades of my life I never saw the sun go down in all its glory. I had nearly ten thousand opportunities, but every opportunity was spent in the pursuit of success.

Success promises that it will make us happy tomorrow, but tomorrow never comes. Even when that moment of achievement arrives, instead of celebrating, we again become anxious to ensure that the celebration is a success. I spent so much time in the Maldives or in Switzerland over these years of achievement, but my mind never enjoyed the waves or the mountains. I was constantly on my laptop or mobile phone, and I sacrificed my happiness for the sake of my success.

Millions around the world are chasing success because they believe in the illusion that 'success is happiness'. Do they achieve a state of happiness by pursuing success from birth to death? Many succeed, but very few achieve a state of peace and bliss. There are people whom I have seen spending years on the success highway, hoping to arrive at the destination happiness, only to realize that it was a mirage. While they spend their life achieving success after success, they sacrifice their life, their relationships, their hobbies and, in the end, their life is full of success, but there is no life left. The promise of happiness only remains like a rainbow in the sky.

'If I had the chance to live my life over again, I would play more golf. I would go to more beaches. I would climb more mountains. I would read more books. I would watch more butterflies and birds. I would sing more songs. I would play more with my children. If only I had my life to live over again, I would not just make money which I earned for others to burn after I depart.' These were a few thoughts shared by a person who regretted living a life spent in pursuit of an illusion: destination success. Most successes have no destination. The destination is death. Instead of enjoying a more fulfilling life, we are accumulating success, money, assets, name and fame, which ultimately will not belong to us. What will we be left with? Regret: we did not do in life what we wished we should have done.

We all know about former heavyweight world champion Mike Tyson's downfall. Over the course of a boxing career that spanned twenty-five years, he earned more than $700 million. And now his net worth is $5 million. His lavish spending habits and the bad advice he had gotten from people he had trusted to help manage his money had depleted his once vast fortune. 'My whole life was a regret. My whole life, my actions, my conduct, a lot of stuff I've done in my life, especially as a fighter,' the man, once nicknamed Iron Mike, had said in an interview with ITV in a show called 'Good Morning Britain'.

If we do not understand what life truly is, and we are enamoured by the illusion that success is happiness, then we will spend our entire life chasing success, even achieving it, but missing true bliss and joy.

Having shut down my business, I try to speak to people, the most successful ones, and I ask them if they are truly happy. Most of them are so drugged by success that they say, 'Yes, I am very excited about what I am doing.' They are consumed by their desire to succeed. Their life is filled with anxiety, and while they enjoy moments of pleasure, they have not even tasted true happiness. Some of them tell me, 'Once I finish this project, I too will call it a day like you and enjoy my life.' It has been years since, but that day has not yet come. I don't think it will ever come. Most successful people are simply blinded by the illusion! Although they know it is an illusion, they believe it to be true and the saddest part is that as the years keep piling they end up devoting their all to just one thing, that is, to ensure that they keep succeeding. It is rather unfortunate that these people would have neither enjoyed peace and tranquility, nor found any meaning and purpose in life. Alas, they would have missed out on those little, yet rare, things that are perhaps more important than sipping the pleasures of success.

TAKEAWAYS

- From the time we are born, we are taught this myth—success is happiness. Unfortunately, this is an illusion.
- Just like the rainbow in the sky, success seems to bring happiness, but it is very momentary.
- We chase success the same way as people in a desert look for the oasis in the distance.
- Those who live with the illusion that success is happiness often end their life in regret. But by then it's too late!

8

SUCCESS CAN MAKE US UNHAPPY

*Success creates money, success creates wealth,
but often, it steals our peace of mind and robs away our health.*

—AiR

While most of the world is seeking success because they believe success is happiness, the truth is that success may or may not give us pleasure, but it is sure to make us unhappy. At the outset, this may seem to be a negative statement, but this is the absolute truth!

In what ways can success make us unhappy? Right from the moment that we desire success till the time we struggle to achieve it, our every step is accompanied by stress and anxiety. If we succeed, we are not excused from worry or anxiety. And if we don't, we are sure to be unhappy. If success is really the cause of unhappiness, then why is the world so enamoured by it?

The unhappiness in success is like a poisonous seed hidden inside a sweet fruit. On the outside, the fruit looks delicious, but as we

SUCCESS CAN MAKE US UNHAPPY

keep biting into it, we taste the bitterness that lies within. Our life could have been lived peacefully and blissfully but, somehow, we bought into the idea that success will give us happiness. We spend our life acquiring skills that will ultimately make us successful. Then we achieve success and with it comes pleasure, name and fame. But we get caught on the roller coaster called success, and by the time we get off, our life is over.

Most success stories are stories of struggle. People often start with nothing and build their empire of success. They become famous and, with the wealth generated by success, they build a home, create financial securities and even send their children to the world's best universities. But what happens to the one who dreamt that success was happiness? At every step, there is so much anxiety. Very often, it is a loan from the bank or from investors who are watching all the time. Sometimes, there is a fear of losing all that took decades to build.

What about those people who are successful politicians? One day, they are everything, and the next, they are nothing. They are so used to being saluted, but their success comes with an expiry date. The rest of their life is spent reminiscing a glory that will never return. Although they may not express it, it is heartbreaking to be in a position of power and enjoy that pleasure only to decline to an ordinary level of life till they depart from the world.

In my journey of success, I never got the time for many things that I wished I did. While I was on the battlefield wishing for victory, there were many unethical things that I had to do, which I now realize only created wealth that ultimately would not belong to me. I suffered through so many legal battles that I had to fight related to my work. There was a phase in my life when I would start at six in the morning and end at midnight—every day of the year, not doing anything productive, but just trying to undo some manipulation done by others in a position of power. Was it worth it, spending years of my life in something so meaningless? I had no choice. If I hadn't, my entire business would have come to a standstill. Those of us who are on this journey called success, are often forced to do things against our will. We just surrender to the circumstances because we don't want to give up success. We suffer the agony that we are forced to face because we don't have the courage to let go of success. We never stop to realize that our life is more important than success.

Most of the unhappiness created by success is subtle and doesn't appear as vividly as success is portrayed. Everybody wants to hear success stories, but nobody has time for failure. Therefore, the subtle pain experienced by those who leave the battlefield of success dissolves into their own misery and goes unnoticed by the world.

There are many people who do not spend their life chasing success. They are happy, far happier than those who spend every moment of their life wanting to win. These people never face the misery and the pain that the successful people face. Their life may be simple and humble, but they are blessed with peace and joy. Prince Siddhartha Gautama, who later became the Buddha or the Awakened One, left his wife and infant son to start his search for the truth. He was not attracted by the wealth that he possessed. One night, he simply left in search of the truth. He did not spend his life chasing success, wealth or pleasures and instead, he was enlightened and realized the truth of lasting peace and bliss.

SUCCESS CAN MAKE US UNHAPPY

TAKEAWAYS

- Success creates a lot of stress and anxiety. It steals our joy.
- The fear of failure too can make us worry and become miserable.
- Successful people, who in time have to vacate their position of power, live with subtle misery that goes unnoticed by the world.
- People who do not pursue success lead a life of contentment peace and joy.

9
THE RACE TO BE AN ACE GETS US CAUGHT IN A MAZE

*We think life is a race, a chase to be an ace.
So, we increase our pace and get caught in a maze.*

—AiR

Most of us in pursuit of success get caught in the race. We want to be an ace, a success, a winner, a champion! Without realizing it, our chase for success and happiness gets us caught in the maze of life. We always thought that success would give us much-desired happiness. We dreamt of enjoying being a winner, so we spent our entire life chasing success.

Why did I jump on to the success train when I was in my teens and then take twenty-five years to pause and reflect? At least I was lucky to stop at forty and contemplate. There are some people who are eighty and are still seeking success, not understanding that their life is soon going to end.

Most successful people in the world enjoy their successes, but they never stop to enjoy life. They enjoy pleasure, but they

THE RACE TO BE AN ACE GETS US CAUGHT IN A MAZE

don't experience peace. A rare minority goes beyond, to find the true purpose of their life. Pleasure is just the first step in the happiness journey. True happiness comes from living in peace, and ultimate happiness comes from finding one's purpose in life. Because success gets us caught in a maze, we struggle through life, enjoying momentary pleasures and soon, it is over.

True success is not just making money, not just earning name and fame, not just being a champion or a winner. True success is discovering our purpose in life. Real happiness comes when we realize the truth of who we are and why we are here. Talk-show queen Oprah Winfrey makes a pertinent point about discovering one's purpose in life: 'Create the highest, grandest vision possible for your life because you become what you believe.'

I was fortunate that I had a life coach, a spiritual master who questioned me about success, happiness and life. First, he made me stop running the race to be an ace when I was forty. He inspired me to shut down my business and to start doing the things that I love. Then, six years later, when he saw that my life was peaceful and blissful, he told me to go on a quest, a search to find the true meaning of life. Today, I feel blessed that I followed his guidance.

Most people in this world live and die thinking that the purpose of life is to be successful. We seek happiness by pursuing success. We achieve success, but true happiness remains a pipe dream. How many people are fortunate to solve the puzzle of life? How many people go on the right path and escape from this maze before they die? A few are fortunate to not get caught in the maze of worldly desires and pleasures; the rest of humanity falls into two categories: the winners and the losers, the successful ones and the failures. Everybody wishes to be a champion, and they start their quest for success—not for the true meaning of their life. People believe that unsuccessful people are miserable. They don't realize that even the successful ones go through enough anxiety and misery.

It's time to stop this mad chase. It's time to realize that life is not a race to be an ace. It's time to get out of this maze, be a true winner: one who is not just successful, but is peaceful and liberated from the stress and anxiety of life, who goes forward to experience true bliss and finds the true purpose and meaning of life.

TAKEAWAYS

- Life is not a race to be an ace. Unfortunately, most of us start the chase to be successful and we get caught in a maze.
- Success only brings momentary and transitory pleasures. It doesn't help us find the true purpose of life.
- Unless we discover true peace, we will not experience real happiness. It's time to stop and seek true happiness.

PART B
THE HAPPINESS JOURNEY

It is sad, but most of us think of happiness as a destination.
This myth makes being a winner, our only motivation.
Those who realize the truth know that happiness is just the path;
happiness is the journey, enjoy it till it lasts.

Do you know what the journey of happiness is all about?
It is living peacefully in the 'now', not letting our mind shout.
It is a choice we must make to be glad, not to be sad,
living with peace, loving every lass and lad.

—AiR

10
WHAT IS TRUE HAPPINESS?

Happiness is simple if we learn to live in the now.
Joy and bliss are possible for those who go with the flow—
it's not in the future, nor in the past, but in the present,
we must realize that happiness is moment by moment.

—AiR

Happiness is a state of being. It is a positive emotion that puts a smile on our face. It is a state of peace and tranquillity. Happiness is different for different people. Such a simple thing like happiness often can't be defined in words. Everybody wants to be happy, but not everybody is. A happy person will laugh, just as an unhappy person may cry. Everybody knows what happiness is, but often, it is misunderstood.

Happiness is not a place that we can go to. Sometimes we think that a product makes us happy. But happiness is not a product. Different things make different people happy, and often, too much of the same thing can even make somebody miserable. Somebody may love to be on a beach, and somebody else may hate to go there. If certain things make one person happy, then those things should make everybody happy. For example, if a cigarette made me happy, then that cigarette should make everybody happy. But this doesn't happen. So, it is not the cigarette that is making us happy. Happiness is already inside us, but different things trigger the happiness that is inside us.

Often, we think that it is a person who gives us happiness. But this also is a misconception. Today somebody may make us happy, but tomorrow, the same person can make us miserable. So, what then is happiness all about?

Happiness is a state of contentment and fulfilment. The Greek philosopher Socrates said: 'He who is not contented with what he has, would not be contented with what he would like to have.' We become happy when we become satisfied. But it is much more. To the common man, happiness is pleasure. Monetary success and material things are the simplest ways to be happy. However, this happiness lasts only for a few moments.

Sometimes, we think that we will be happy tomorrow. But happiness doesn't exist in the future. It is all about the present moment. Our quest for happiness starts when we are children. Even a child can be happy or unhappy. Give the child his favourite toy and you will find him smiling and laughing. Take away the toy, and the child will instantly scream and cry. The desire for happiness is instinctive. No human being wants to be unhappy. Till our last breath, we seek happiness.

Different things make different people happy. A teacher is happy when his students fare well in an examination. A singer is happy when their song is a hit. A manufacturer is happy when his product is popular. A sportsman is happy when he wins a game. Everybody's happiness comes from a different source of fulfilment. What makes me happy need not make you happy. Despite happiness being an individual thing, somehow we believe that happiness comes

WHAT IS TRUE HAPPINESS?

from achievement. We have discussed this at length: success is not happiness.

Don't you want to be happy? For sure! Like anybody else, you are reading this book because you want to be happy. It is absolutely normal for a human being to seek joy. While the whole world wants to be happy, not everybody is. But there are some people who seem to be happier than others. What is the secret of their happiness?

Anybody can be happy. You don't need to be a millionaire or a world champion to be happy. Kelly Catlin, an American professional racing cyclist, won gold medals in various world championships. Even after achieving success, she committed suicide months after suffering a concussion due to a cycling accident. This is not the only case. There are several other such instances where so-called 'successful' people have ended their life. This is because life is not just about being successful. To live happily, you need the correct thought process. Whoever you are, wherever you live and whatever you do, there is a way to be happy. To some, the way to happiness may be easy and for others it may be a struggle.

Aleksandr 'Schoolboy' Beziazykov of Russia broke his arm in an accident when he was seven years old. Doctors said he would never be able to pursue his passion of becoming an Olympic athlete again because of the nerve damage and improper joint fusion after the surgery. He had to quit athletics because of this. He had a dream to become an Olympic champion in track and field, but he was unable to participate in any sporting activities for two years. At the age of fifteen, he got back to the gym and switched from track and field athletics to arm wrestling, and the more he started winning, the more he loved this sport. He is now able to travel around the world because of it and compete amongst the best.

Happiness is living with faith, hope, trust and enthusiasm. It is eliminating fear that can paralyse us. Over the last eighteen months, between 2020 and 2021, the fear of death and disease caused by the coronavirus has corroded people's happiness across the globe. People are living with the dreaded 'coronaphobia', and this has stolen their happiness. What can we do about the virus? We can wear a mask, keep social distance, but can we control what happens in a laboratory in Wuhan? We must learn to surrender, to accept and to move on if we truly want to be happy.

Happiness is a choice. You cannot choose what happens, but you can choose your reaction to it.

TAKEAWAYS

- Happiness doesn't exist in the future. It is all about the present moment.
- The desire for happiness is instinctive. No human being wants to be unhappy.
- Happiness is a state of being. It is not a product, a place or a person.
- We don't have to be a successful millionaire to be happy. Anybody can be happy. Happiness is a choice. To be happy, we must learn to accept, surrender and live with enthusiasm.

11

DO YOU KNOW WHAT MAKES YOU HAPPY?

How can we be happy if we don't even know what makes us happy? Stop! And make your happiness list now!

—AiR

While everybody wants to be happy, it is strange that most people don't really know what makes them happy. We cannot be happy unless we are aware of what gives us joy, peace and bliss.

Like everyone else, I too have been seeking happiness since childhood. Today, I am truly happy. I have made this a part of my life's mission to help people live a life of eternal happiness and everlasting peace. My own happiness came from reaching out to the poor and needy. I would go out every night and give them packets of food or blankets. This made me happy. I used one of my quotes and had it printed on stress balls, 'If you can be glad but you choose to be sad, you are mad', and I share it with as many people as I can. After all, isn't happiness the goal of our life? My objective has been simple: to inspire people to be happy. As my life evolved, I started writing books on happiness and even gave talks on happiness.

In my quest for happiness, I met several people and asked them a simple question, 'Do you know what makes you happy?' Most of them fumbled, and while they knew some things that made them happy, it took them quite some time to list things that truly made them happy. Can you list ten things that make you happy? Chances are you won't be able to! Because most of us want to be happy, but we don't know what makes us happy.

I also made pocket-sized cards and distributed them to people. It was titled 'My Happiness List'. I encouraged people to carry this with them at all times and note down things or activities that make them happy. I called these 'happiness triggers'.

What could some of your happiness triggers be? It could be listening to a favourite song or talking to your best friend or eating your favourite food or simply going for a walk. For some people, it is not a walk but a long drive, just as for others it is not a friend but a pet that makes them happy. I know people who are not foodies, but a drink does put a smile on their face. Whatever makes you happy, should be in your happiness list. If you don't know what makes you happy, then you may slip into a state of unhappiness and depression every now and then.

The first step to finding happiness is finding out what makes us happy, for if we don't know what makes us happy, how will we ever be joyous? If we really want to be happy then we will make it a habit to pull happiness triggers whenever we feel like being happy.

When I started my happiness journey, I was sure that I didn't want any more achievements to give me happiness. I tried to find out what really makes me happy. I got myself a pet dog. My pet dog gave me far more happiness than I got from all the pleasures in so many years.

I knew that serving the poor gave me great joy and peace, so I put that in my happiness list. Watching a beautiful sunrise or sunset made my heart dance with joy, just like singing bhajans did. Once I created my happiness list and started pulling these happiness triggers, my life was transformed into one of peace, joy and bliss.

However, when I tried to make others happy, I found that they were prisoners of things that made them unhappy. I tried to make them realize the importance of drawing on happiness triggers by first making their 'happiness list'. All those who did it found this to be life-changing. Whenever they found a shadow of unhappiness, they would pick one or two of the happiness triggers and pull at them. They realized that, after all, happiness was not such a difficult thing. It was a choice, and we, human beings, can choose to be happy.

TAKEAWAYS

- If we want to be happy, we must know what makes us happy.
- Unfortunately, most people don't know what triggers happiness in their life.
- People should make a list of happiness triggers to find out what truly makes them happy.
- Listing what makes us happy and pulling on the happiness triggers are steps towards being happy.

12
HAPPINESS IS A CHOICE

Happiness is a choice,
but this is known only to the wise.
Happy and sad, like a pendulum, we swing,
and in our life, miseries we bring.

—AiR

Happiness doesn't depend on what you have, but rather on how you feel. That is because happiness is a choice. Most of the world does not realize this truth. We are seeking pleasure, people, possessions and are even going to places to be happy. But we are never happy. Even if we get what we want, we are only happy for that moment. Soon, we start craving for something else. We don't realize that the fulfilment of these desires will never quench our thirst. They ultimately make us burst with disappointment.

I too, had a choice. Today, I live a happy life because I made a conscious choice to be happy. I don't let anyone or anything steal my happiness, just like I consciously do things that make me happy.

Most people are unable to remain happy because they don't know how to be happy. They are unable to choose happiness because they have not learned the art of happiness. But there are some people who constantly live a life of bliss and joy. Hollywood actress Drew Barrymore makes an interesting observation: 'I think happiness is a choice. If you feel yourself being happy and can settle into the life choices you make, then it's great. It's really, really great. I swear to God, happiness is the best makeup.'

I learned this valuable lesson many decades ago from one of the managers of our stores and a distant relative—Chellaram. He was a humble man and had hardly any wealth or possessions to brag about. Still, he was always smiling. His cheerfulness was contagious. Whoever he met, he would give them a broad smile and laugh cheerfully. He had this habit of telling people, 'Be happy always. Be cheerful.' What made Chellaram such a happy man? He lived in a very small home and nothing in his life was beyond the ordinary. Still, he was so blissful. Was it because he spent most of his life reaching out to the unfortunate and helping them? That was part of his daily morning schedule. But after that he lived a normal life. He went to work and came back to his family. Still, he was uniquely happy.

I realized that Chellaram made happiness a choice. Every day, he resolved that he would be happy, just as he made sure he would never be unhappy.

We human beings are strange. We know very well what makes us happy. But we permit the unhappiness song to repeatedly play throughout our life. Some of us, despite knowing what makes us happy, do not pull on the happiness triggers.

We must consciously make a choice to be happy. We must be convinced of the fact that it is contentment and not achievement that makes us blissful. We must want both—to be happy and do things that make us happy. Above all, we must learn to live with contentment. Just like anything else in the world, happiness too is an art that we must develop. Make a choice to be happy today and every day that you live.

Today, you can choose to live with faith or to live with fear. You can let a little virus stop you from living with a smile as it hides your laughter behind the mask or you can wear a mask, but not let it affect your peace and bliss. After all, nothing is more important than happiness.

TAKEAWAYS

- Happiness is a choice. We must choose to be happy.
- Most people are unable to remain happy because they haven't learned the art of happiness.
- True happiness doesn't depend on what you have, but rather depends on how you feel.
- Happiness comes from contentment, not from achievement.
- We must want both—to be happy and to do things that make us happy.
- We can choose to live with fear or with faith. It's our choice!

13

FLIP OVER FROM NEP TO PEP

PEP is Positive Energy Power,
NEP is Negative Energy Poison.
If you flip your life over, from NEP to PEP,
there will only be peace and joy on the horizon.

—AiR

As we live, our life is filled with thoughts, thoughts that are both positive and negative. We have always been advised to think positive. I too wanted to 'think positive', but I struggled as I could not control my negative thoughts. I spent years in the analysis of positive thinking and was blessed to discover the secret.

Our mind is like a thought factory. It keeps on producing thoughts. Just like any factory, it needs raw material to produce thought. Emotions provide the raw material. Whatever emotions we feed our mind with, chances are it will produce those thoughts.

If we fill our mind with positive emotions like courage, confidence, faith, hope, enthusiasm, love, peace, joy, compassion, forgiveness, kindness and optimism, then our thought factory or our mind will produce positive thoughts.

However, if we fill our mind with negative emotions like fear, worry, hate, anger, jealousy, revenge, pessimism, doubt and the like, then our mind will constantly produce negative thoughts. As Charlie Chaplin once said, 'You'll never find a rainbow if you're looking down.'

Why does this happen? It is because our thought factory works on the principle of Negative Energy Poison (NEP) and Positive Energy Power (PEP). Negative energy has poison, just as positive energy has power. If we want to live a happy life, we must learn to flip over and switch from NEP to PEP. How does one do that? If we let negative emotions into our life, which is a conscious choice most of the time, then our mind will keep on producing unhappy thoughts. NEP cannot produce happy thoughts. Negative emotions are poisonous and because the raw material is poison, the product of the mind—thoughts—will be miserable. As Michael Jordan once said, 'Always turn a negative situation into a positive situation.'

However, positive thoughts make us happy. If we don't choose positive emotions consciously, the mind will choose negative emotions by default. To be happy, we must consciously choose PEP, the raw material of positive energy, just as we must resolve never to let NEP or negative emotions enter our life.

Look around you and you will find this everywhere. People who are living with fear, worry, hate, jealousy and anger are unhappy. But people who are living with courage, confidence, forgiveness, love and faith are joyous. This is no magic. There is simple logic to it, which I have explained. It is a principle but because people don't know it, it remains a secret. Decode this principle, fill your life with PEP, just as you empty NEP from your life and you will find happy thoughts—a source of your happiness.

When I discovered the secret of NEP and PEP, I realized something very profound. Whenever I was free, negative emotions would flow into my life. It seemed that as if by default my mind was producing negative thoughts. I further realized that thoughts are the beginning of the chain of happiness or unhappiness. Thoughts lead to feelings, feelings to actions, actions become habits, and habits create our character, which finally decides our destiny. Therefore, if we do not choose PEP, NEP slowly sinks into our life and then there is no way we can live a happy life.

Therefore, the secret is to switch from NEP to PEP. Every time NEP entered, I would flip over to PEP. If doubt came, I would flip over to faith. If there was fear, I would replace it with courage. The only way to remove hate was to bring in love. It was a conscious effort, but every negative emotion needed to be flipped over. If I felt revengeful, the flip happened with forgiveness. This flipping was magical because it was the raw material of my thought factory. As I kept feeding my mind with positive emotions through a conscious choice, I eliminated negative emotions from it, I found that my life became a life of PEP. There was a positive energy in my life, and I was able to think positively. This was one practical solution that I discovered to create happiness.

The world today is gripped by NEP. We are controlled by FEAR—a False Expectation Appearing Real. Fear of death and disease has spread into every cell of every human being, so much so that countries have shut their borders and it has brought the world to a standstill. Unfortunately, NEP has got the better of PEP and has stolen our peace and bliss. Mahatma Gandhi rightly said, 'More people die out of the fear of the disease than of the disease itself.' Are we going to let NEP get the better of us or are we going to flip over to PEP, and switch from fear to faith, from misery to bliss?

TAKEAWAYS

- Emotions are the raw material of the thought factory, our mind.
- Whatever we feed our mind with, our thoughts will echo.
- If we fill our life with positive emotions like courage, confidence, faith, hope, enthusiasm, love, peace, joy, compassion, forgiveness, kindness and optimism, we will have positive thoughts, making way for us to be be happy.
- But if we let negative emotions like fear, worry, hate, anger, jealousy, revenge, pessimism and doubt sink in, we are bound to have negative thoughts and thus be unhappy.
- If you want to be happy, switch to Positive Energy Power (PEP) from Negative Energy Poison (NEP).

14

THE MAGIC OF CONTENTMENT AND FULFILMENT

*There can be no smoke without fire,
there can be no misery without desire.*

—AiR

It is largely believed that success brings happiness, but this is not happiness; it is pleasure. Still, the whole world is out seeking achievement. Thus, we live like we are strung on a yo-yo. Sometimes we are happy and sometimes we are unhappy. While pleasure gives us momentary happiness, it is peace that creates tranquillity, on which our happiness is built. How does one achieve peace?

As long as we are chasing achievement, we are living with stress, worry and anxiety. This robs us of our peace. It destroys the very foundation of our happiness. Therefore, we have to move away from stress and anxiety. This comes with contentment.

Contentment is a state of being fully satisfied. It is being happy, fulfilling our need and not letting greed be a master of our life. The moment we let desire and craving create a passion, we will never be satisfied. There will be no contentment and there will be no peace. We can never build lasting happiness without peace. One of the Four Noble Truths shared by Buddha was that *desire* and attachment are at the *root of all suffering*.

When we take an exit from the highway of achievement, we realize that happiness is a journey, not a destination. We learn to enjoy the journey called happiness and we live with contentment.

Contentment is just the start. If we want to evolve through the happiness journey, contentment must become fulfilment, which includes living with a universal divine connection and working towards a life of liberation and freedom. Fulfilment needs faith just as it needs inspiration. Then, there is laughter and love that fills our life. We start a new journey, living with meaning and purpose. Our priority is not making money but making a difference. Of course, it is all about being positive. Some people worry about how life could be lived without motivation and success. Living with fulfilment means noteworthy success, but it is not a life which aims only for success and nothing else. Finally, fulfilment is all about living with tranquillity and peace. The word can be broken down as follows:

FULFILMENT

F : Full satisfaction and contentment
U : Universal connection
L : Liberation and freedom
F : Faith, hope and surrender
I : Inspiration, energy and enthusiasm
L : Living with meaning and purpose
M : Making a difference
E : Emotionally positive
N : Noteworthy success and achievement
T : Tranquillity and peace

THE MAGIC OF CONTENTMENT AND FULFILMENT

Being fulfilled is to live with peace, joy and bliss. Everybody in this world faces misery and sorrow. Is there a way to escape it? And then, there is the problem of shuttling between the past and the future. Is there a way out of this?

TAKEAWAYS

- Peace can be achieved if we live a life of contentment.
- Contentment is the beginning of a state of fulfilment.
- Fulfilment promises a life of peace, joy and bliss.
- We must follow the acronym of fulfilment to live with peace and tranquillity.

15

HAPPINESS EXISTS IN THE 'NOW'

Think of today, not tomorrow.
It's time to be happy! Don't live a life of sorrow.
Find out those things that make you glad,
and eliminate those that make you sad.

—AiR

Those who want to be happy must understand an important truth about happiness: we can neither be happy in a yesterday that is gone nor can we be happy in a tomorrow that is not yet born.If we want to be happy, we have to be happy 'now'! This means that we must live in the present moment. The moment we lose the 'now', we lose happiness.

It is very natural for us to slip into our past. Our mind takes us to scenes not only of yesterday and last week, but also to incidents that happened years ago. Very often, when we remember something that hurt us—we nurse it, we curse it and we rehearse it in our memory. We are not able to shut the door on those miserable memories and forget them once and for all.

One of my uncles, let me call him Uncle Misery, lived abroad.

HAPPINESS EXISTS IN THE 'NOW'

Whenever he visited India and met me, he would say, 'When I visited the last time, you didn't bother to come and meet me.' Then he would continue, 'Last year, I requested you to give me your car to go to the airport, and you refused.' He further continued, 'Three years ago, I wanted the electrician to repair my geyser and you did not help.' He never stopped! He would go on, 'When my daughter was six years old (now she is sixteen), she needed to go to the doctor, and you did not take her to the doctor!'

Uncle Misery lived in the past. He was always miserable. Luckily, I had learned the art of not listening to such garbage. I did not let these become a memory that would later on haunt me and make me feel miserable. Uncle Misery shows us how easy it is to lose our moments of joy when we slip into the past.

The problem is not only about the past. We often swing into the future and live with constant fear. What is FEAR? It is False Expectations Appearing Real. Those who live in the future undergo stress, worry and anxiety. The future has not yet unfolded, but we let our fears take charge, which makes us worry and creates stress. And, our life is filled with anxiety. How can we then be happy?

Once, when I was visiting a friend, a business magnate, his secretary called him to inform that the police had come downstairs with a warrant. My friend panicked and said, 'Why has the police come? What are they going to do with me? What will happen if they arrest me and put me in jail? What will happen to my family? In jail, if there is no good food, I will become sick. Who will take care of me when I am with all the criminals and murderers in jail?' By swinging into the future, my friend had created loads of misery and suffering for himself. It was only when he came down and met the police that he realized that it was not him that the police were looking for, but his namesake who lived four blocks away. What was my friend guilty of? He was guilty of losing the present moment of peace and joy and of slipping into a future that was unreal.

Why do people say that tomorrow never comes? It is because tomorrow can never come. It can only come as 'today'. When 'tomorrow' becomes 'today', we will have enough power and courage to face it, so we must learn to close the door tightly on tomorrow.

If we want to be happy, we must stop this constant shuttling between our past and our future. Unfortunately, for most of us, that is unavoidable. One moment we are in the past, and the next moment we are in the future. We fail to live in the present moment, and we don't realize that happiness is in the 'now'. Happiness belongs to this moment. If we lose this moment, then we lose this opportunity of being happy. Today, the world has lost its biggest gift—the present. People are living with the fear of COVID-19 and are pondering over the Spanish flu that devastated the world a hundred years ago. Then, we are jumping into the future. What if we get infected by the coronavirus? What if we are in a hospital bed without a ventilator? What if we die? Why jump from the past to the future? Why not live in the present moment? Why not count our blessings that all is good today, and all will be good tomorrow? Why not live life moment by moment, day by day, with a smile and with laughter and sing the song,

Que sera, sera,
whatever will be, will be...
the future's not ours to see!
que sera, sera,
what will be, will be...

—Jay Livingston and Ray Evans

HAPPINESS EXISTS IN THE 'NOW'

In my journey of life, I have realized that life is made up of years, months and days. Days are made up of hours, minutes and moments. If we lose the moment, we lose life.

I find it both amusing and unfortunate when I see people on a beautiful beach busy on their laptops. As I snorkel and enjoy the divine underwater world, blissful and peaceful as each moment passes, these people lose the moment. They destroy the 'now'! And then they ask me, 'How can we be happy?'

TAKEAWAYS

- Happiness belongs to the 'now'.
- When we slip into the past or swing to the future, we lose the present moment of joy.
- If we want to be happy, we must stop shuttling between our past and our future.
- We must live blissfully and peacefully in the 'now'.

16
MIND: THE BIGGEST ENEMY OF HAPPINESS

Why do we suffer in life, do you know?
Why do our stress and anxiety grow?
Because our mind jumps from the future to the past,
The joy that is ours just doesn't last.

—AiR

While we are all seeking happiness, we must know who it is that steals our happiness. Who is the enemy of our joy and bliss? You will be surprised to know that the enemy is our own mind.

The uncontrolled mind is a rascal. It is like a naughty monkey. It keeps jumping from the past to the future, from one thought to another. By doing so, it steals away our present moment of peace and joy. This is not the only thing that it does. It does many other things that become the main cause of our unhappiness. Unless we are able to tame our mind, tie it down and bring it under our control, we can never be happy. Lord Hanuman symbolizes the mind that has become disciplined and is filled with devotion. Hanuman is the evolved state of our unruly mind that constantly jumps from thought to thought.

The mind is constantly producing thoughts. It is producing up to 50,000 thoughts a day. It practically produces one thought every second. It is this constant production of thought that is the main cause of our stress and anxiety. If we want to overcome this misery, we must learn to slow down our mind. We must learn to reduce the MTR—the Mental Thought Rate. We must pin down the monkey and contemplate a single thought so that our mind is not constantly jumping from one random thought to another. This is often referred to as meditation. Unfortunately, the world doesn't understand its true meaning. The focus is solely on sitting in a particular posture, keeping our spine erect and closing our eyes. Despite attaining a perfect posture, if the monkey mind is constantly jumping from thought to thought, is it meditation? True meditation is being conscious of the activity of the mind. In modern parlance, it is called 'mindfulness', which in reality means emptying the mind. Unless we are able to control our mind, we can never live a happy life.

The mind likes to dwell on negative emotions. Unless we consciously fill our life with positive emotions, it will, by default, create fear. It makes us worry, just as it makes us angry. All these negative emotions constantly create negative thoughts. The mind jumps into the past and makes us regret something that we did years ago. We know that we can do nothing about it, but still our mind takes us into that domain of regret and misery. The mind triggers thoughts of revenge and hate and provokes us to get angry.

Today, what is on top of our minds? As we watch people wearing masks in the COVID-19 scenario, the mind triggers fear of the disease and of death. Although coronavirus has been around for the past two years, it has not caused fatalities like the Spanish flu, which it is being compared to. Still, the pandemic has created pandemonium in the mind. This is because the mind makes the wolf bigger than it is. It can inflate a problem and make an imaginary fear look like a real danger. Unless we tame our monkey mind, it will continue to make us suffer. There is only one solution: tame the monkey mind into a monk, remove all the junk from it, and learn to live with happiness.

It was my spiritual guru who blessed me with this wisdom. Many years ago, I went to him, fuming about how a person who I considered loyal had cheated me. I wanted to report him to the police, block his bank account and hurt him in as many ways as I could. My mind was very agitated. My guru taught me the art of using my intellect. He said, 'Whatever has been done, is done. Whatever you will do now will only further your misery. Remember that the hand that wants to throw burning coals on others to hurt them will first burn itself.' He taught me to activate my intellect to control my mind from doing anything that would cause further misery. He also made me realize that I cannot control people's actions, but I can control my reaction. He further explained how we have five senses that are like the five horses leading a chariot—our body. These horses of our life are controlled by reins. The rein is our mind. If we want to have control over our life, then we must be like the charioteer who controls the horses. If we don't use our intellect to control the mind, which controls our senses, then our five senses will go wild, much like the five horses and take our life in all undesired directions.

In the Bhagavad Gita, Lord Krishna tells Arjun, 'O mighty-armed Arjun, subdue the self (senses, mind, and intellect) by the self (strength of the soul), and kill this formidable enemy called lust.'

I learned that I must control my mind if I wanted to achieve

MIND: THE BIGGEST ENEMY OF HAPPINESS

true happiness. I was the master of my life and my happiness, and my biggest enemy, my own mind, was constantly doing things to make me unhappy. Unless I was conscious that my mind is a rascal, I would continue to follow it and my life would end in sorrow.

The mind, however, is an intelligent rascal. It makes us believe it is the king, it is everything. There are people who believe that they are nothing without the mind. 'I think, therefore I am' is a very famous quote by the great French philosopher René Descartes. But the truth is: '*I am, therefore I think*'. First, we are the divine soul or the life energy and our mind is just a part of our body. Since people live in ignorance and they do not know the difference between the mind and the intellect, they believe that the mind is the supreme aspect of our existence. But the mind is that domain of our subtle existence that produces thoughts. The intellect discriminates between what is right and wrong. We must make our intellect the master of our mind. We must use our intellect to make wise choices. If we let the mind be our master, we are surely doomed to live a life of unhappiness.

TAKEAWAYS

- The mind is a rascal. It is our biggest enemy. It makes us unhappy.
- The mind is like a monkey, constantly jumping from thought to thought.
- If we want to be happy, we must slow down our mind.
- Happiness belongs to those who make the intellect the master of the mind.
- If we don't control our mind, we are sure to be unhappy.

17

PEACE IS THE FOUNDATION OF BLISS

*Happiness is not money,
or the fame you get after a chase.
Happiness is the peace and tranquillity,
that puts a smile on your face.*

—AiR

Have you ever seen happiness grow without a foundation of peace? Where there is no peace, there can be no happiness. Still, people seek happiness without creating peace in their life. It is ironic that we give up peace for the sake of happiness.

Happiness is not just about instant gratification. These pleasures come and go. Everlasting happiness needs peace and tranquillity. Each of our senses is constantly seeking pleasures. The eyes see, the nose smells, the ears listen, the tongue tastes and the skin touches. Each of these sensations triggers the mind to desire and seek pleasure. It may be food, perfume or simple music. All these are momentary. They come and go. We can enjoy these pleasures—provided our mind is peaceful. If there is turbulence within, then none of these sensations will give us pleasure. Can you enjoy good music when the mind is stressed? Impossible! The mind must be still.

What is peace? It is freedom from disturbance. What causes this disturbance? It is ME—the Mind and Ego. The mind craves and desires, creating turbulence. Before this, there was peace and bliss, but the rascal, ME, robbed our peace by this craving and desire. Even after we achieve some peace, we only return to the original state of peace. We lost our peace in that duration, and we seem so happy to return to our original state of tranquillity. There is a constant war within us. The ME is constantly looking out at the world to fulfil certain expectations. When those expectations are not fulfilled, we become disappointed, discouraged and defeated. Only if we learn to stop the ME from this rumbling and mumbling in the material world can we have peace and enjoy happiness.

Haven't you experienced the ego getting angry and upset when it expects something and it is not fulfilled? Along with the mind, the ego makes our happiness dissolve by destroying our peace and tranquillity.

When I was chasing my dreams and goals, I used to write an obsession statement every year. Somehow, I was passionate to achieve what I set out to. Most often I did, but what was the price I paid? I gave up my peace for the sake of achieving my dream. Although I made my dream come true, and I celebrated it, there was no 'true' happiness because there was no peace.

Being peaceful is a prerequisite for being blissful. Despite possessing wealth and fame, if one has no tranquillity, then one can never enjoy true happiness. Peace is the foundation of happiness, for if there is no peace, happiness cannot exist. We human beings do not give enough value to peace. Thus, we find it strange when we are told of a simple way to be happy. Just spend fifteen minutes every morning and every evening in silence and this can change your life. When my mentor told me this, I actually laughed. How can just doing nothing and being silent create happiness?

'Isn't it a waste of time?' I asked him.

My mentor laughed and questioned me, 'Do you pay your security guard to sit outside in silence and do nothing?'

'Of course not!' I replied. 'He may be sitting in silence, but he is watching. That is his job.'

The master replied, 'Good, you too must sit in silence and observe the mind as it jumps, the ego as it cries. Your simple act of observing the mind will give you the much-desired peace and happiness that you seek.'

What is it that robs our peace of mind? How can we be peaceful and blissful? We must resolve to make our peace our priority. Suppose something is happening in the world—like a pandemic, a natural disaster or a humanitarian crisis—it must not affect our peace. We must learn to watch whatever is unfolding as a divine drama. We must do our part in protecting ourselves and be compassionate towards others in whatever way we can. But, under no circumstances should we lose our peace of mind. If we do, we will sink into gloom and doom.

TAKEAWAYS

- Where there is no peace, happiness cannot exist.
- Sometimes we wonder how being peaceful and silent can help, but we do not realize its value.
- When we are peaceful, ME, the Mind and the Ego, slows down, and this reduces our stress and anxiety.
- Peace creates consistent bliss and joy. It is very different from pleasure, which is momentary.

18
DISCOVER THE RAINBOW OF 'TRUE' LOVE

True love is of the soul,
it is our ultimate goal.
When souls together twine,
it is eternal love that's divine.

—AiR

One of the pieces of the happiness puzzle is love. Don't we all know that love creates joy? But unfortunately, we don't know the meaning of true love. If we want bliss, then we must not think that love is just a kiss. Love is one of the most powerful emotions gifted to man. It arrives from the moment we are born and is with us till we die. Still, we don't realize that it is not the body that loves, but the divinity that is alive within.

True love is like a rainbow. It is made up of seven colours: Violet, Indigo, Blue, Green, Yellow, Orange and Red—VIBGYOR. Violet love is between parents and children. Doesn't this give true joy? Indigo love is between friends. I remember the days of my childhood where happiness was all about friendship. Blue love is romance. Lovers feel their heart dance with joy when romance fills the air. Green love is love for oneself. Sometimes, it is our love of self that gives us fulfilment. Yellow love is intellectual love. It is love between two people on an intellectual platform. There is so much happiness that people can have during an intellectual interaction. Orange love is emotional love, love that is more feminine, that goes from heart to heart, creating bliss and joy. Red love is the love that is famous—it is erotic love, love that is all about hearts, kisses and hugs. It is physical love, which is just one of the colours of the rainbow but it seems to overpower the other colours of love. But this too creates an ocean of happiness.

All these seven manifestations of love provide a different kind of excitement, bliss and happiness, but we have still not found the source of love. Pure love is white in colour. It is divine love that comes from the soul and leads to eternal bliss and happiness. Very few people are lucky to discover this source of love. Just like a rainbow appears when the white light of the sun shines through droplets of water, so also white love from the soul manifests as the seven colours of love and flows like a fountain of divine bliss from birth until death.

Those who find this piece of the puzzle, fill their life with bliss. They go beyond the red, erotic love and enjoy all the seven colours of love, each colour bringing into their life a different flavour of happiness. Those who misunderstand love are deprived of this bliss and only enjoy a tiny portion of physical or emotional love wherein happiness too appears, but in bits and pieces.

We are shy even to say 'I love you', because we don't discover the true, divine meaning of love. The connection of love and happiness can be traced back to thousands of years ago in the temples of India where erotic love has been sculpted on the walls or the facade of the temples.

There is a divine power within each one of us. The power that gives life itself. It is this power that is, in reality, expressing love to the same power that is in the beloved and, in fact, is everywhere. This has deep divine significance, but very few people are fortunate to realize this. While I realized the power of white divine love, the least I can share is how the seven colours of love, together remembered as the rainbow, bring happiness into our life at every stage that we live through. We must not miss this happiness and we must enjoy the seven colours of the rainbow of love.

TAKEAWAYS

- True love is bliss. It manifests as the seven colours of the rainbow.
- Violet love is family love, Indigo love is friendly love, Blue love is romantic love, Green love is self-love, Yellow love is intellectual love, Orange love is emotional love and Red love is erotic love.
- True love is white in colour. It is divine soulful love.
- Without the white light from the sun, there would be no rainbow. For the seven colours of love to appear, we need white divine love.
- From the time we are born till the time we die, love manifests at every step and fills our life with joy and bliss.
- Because we do not discover what true love is, we miss the bliss of true love.

19
A SMILE DOESN'T COST ANYTHING

*You can be happy all the time,
if you learn to smile and not whine.
Don't jump from the future to the past,
be in the now and make happiness last.*

—AiR

What does it cost to give somebody a smile? Nothing! But stop and look around you. How many people are smiling? Why don't people smile? It is an instant way to be happy and to make others happy. Although we know this, we hardly smile.

Sometimes, it seems that the world really doesn't want to be happy. If people actually wanted happiness, we would make a conscious effort to smile at others. Doctors today talk about several health benefits of smiling. Not only does a smile create a good, happy mood, it also helps release endorphins that are said to lead to reduced blood pressure, pain and stress. It increases our endurance and strengthens our immune system.

A SMILE DOESN'T COST ANYTHING

More and more people are advocating the importance of smiling and laughing. Together, they trigger movements of facial muscles, which trigger the brain to release certain chemicals, hormones and neurotransmitters, including dopamine and serotonin that are said to be directly connected to our happiness levels as they reduce our stress levels. Still, we hardly smile and laugh!

Many years ago, it was popularly believed that when you are happy, you will smile or laugh. Norman Vincent Peale, known as the father of positive thinking, reversed the belief and said that if you smile and laugh, you can be happy. While the world knows that happiness makes us smile, it is worth trying to smile and create joy. You will see that a smile makes you happy.

In my pursuit of happiness, I have distributed over 100,000 smiley balls with a happiness quote on each of them. The ball instantly fosters a smile and thus spreads happiness. Since making people happy is part of my life mission, I often compliment flight attendants and tell them that they look good when they smile. This always has the desired effect; suddenly, they start smiling even more and thus radiate happiness to everybody in the flight.

While we want to be happy, we sometimes underestimate the power of a smile. Try to go to a very serious-looking person today and give them a smile and you will find instant happiness glowing through their smile. A smile doesn't cost anything, still it is priceless. I believe this: more important than being a millionaire is being a 'smile millionaire', one who makes it a point to give a smile to everyone they meet. Happiness is a simple thing. Somehow, we have complicated it. We think we need an expensive car or a vacation to an exotic location to be happy. Some people wait to eat an imported lobster to bring a smile on their faces. But in reality, we can smile without any of these things. Anyone can smile. Anyone, from any nation, any culture, any religion, any gender, any age—there is no restriction on anyone to smile.

TAKEAWAYS

- While the whole world wants to be happy, not many people use a simple thing like a smile to radiate happiness.
- While a smile costs nothing, why are we so stingy when it comes to giving somebody a smile?
- Smiling and laughter are said to have direct benefits on our body and mind. They release certain chemicals and hormones that improve our state of happiness and reduce our stress levels.
- A smile not only evokes happiness for the one who gives it, but also for the one who receives it. Give someone a smile today!

20

THE SIMPLE SECRET TO HAPPINESS

*To be happy and to make others happy,
are the two best things to do in life.*

—AiR

If you really want to be happy, then you must learn this one secret that is guaranteed to give you happiness: *make others happy and you are sure to become happy yourself*. Do you want to try this simple secret? Stop doing whatever you are doing now and spend the next two hours making people happy. What can you do? You can compliment the first person you meet by telling them that they look pretty, or that they have some amazing quality. A compliment can easily make somebody happy. The moment you make them happy, you will realize that happiness is reflective. It beams back to us. Take a few chocolates and distribute them to a few people and also wish them an amazing day. Chances are you will find a very positive response and happiness will return to you like a boomerang. The happiness that goes around, comes around.

Surprise a friend with a call and say something good. Call somebody and thank them profusely for doing something nice for you in the past. There are many ways to make people happy. Find out more and more ways. The secret is the more you make others happy, the happier you become. Try it, and you will discover a new happiness secret.

I discovered this secret thirty-five years ago. From the first monetary success that I achieved, I took out a share and made food packets to distribute among homeless people. They were labourers who were going to sleep hungry. They were surprised when I patted their back and offered them a warm meal. They not only thanked me, but also blessed me. I have never experienced such joy in my life. I continued this exercise and instead of doing it every Monday, I tried doing it twice a week. I found so many people suffering on the streets and I tried to help them in every way I could. I personally distributed thousands of blankets among destitutes. Every time I made them happy, I was creating multifolds of happiness for myself. To them, I was a godsend. Nobody ever before had come and showered love on them. Months of driving through the streets made me discover this profound but simple happiness secret—if you want to be happy, make others happy.

Since then, I have never lost an opportunity to make others happy. I find that it works in more ways than one. Firstly, the act of making others happy instantly creates joy. The hand that gives the rose retains some of its fragrance. The recipients of the kind act express their gratitude, which causes another stream of happiness. When I was blessed with prayers, it created bliss that had no price tag. However, it was much later that I realized something greater: every time I performed an act of making others happy, I was creating positive karma. Karma means action. There is a universal law of action and reaction, popularly known as the law of karma. The law proclaims, 'What you give is what you get.' In a simple interpretation of the law, if you spread happiness, you will get happiness.

THE SIMPLE SECRET TO HAPPINESS

Those who are serious about the happiness journey must give a lot of importance to this simple secret because, in reality, it is the greatest law of happiness. What does this law teach us? It teaches us that bad things can't happen to good people, just as apples can't grow on mango trees. Have you seen a mango tree laden with apples? 'Impossible!' you would say. 'How can a mango tree bear apples?' This is a universal law. The law states, 'As you sow, so shall you reap.' If you plant coconuts, you will get coconuts and not jackfruit. Therefore, if bad things seem to be happening to good people, it is because they have done something bad in the past. There is no way to escape our actions. Remember, it is not necessary that only the one whom you make happy will return happiness. The natural law with its universal powers will ensure that happiness is constantly showered on you.

With this comes a more profound learning. It starts with making others happy but goes further, and is about doing good to others. The more good you do, the more good will return to you. This is a universal law and you cannot escape it. Therefore, if you want fruits of happiness, you must plant seeds of happiness. If you want joy, bliss, peace and goodness to come to you, live a life being good to others, spreading joy, bliss and peace, and you will find your life full of happiness.

TAKEAWAYS

- If you want to be happy, make others happy.
- Happiness that goes around, comes around.
- It starts with this simple tenet but goes much deeper to become the universal law of karma.
- The law states, 'As you sow, so shall you reap.'
- If you plant happy deeds, you will reap happy fruits.
- Your happiness is ultimately in your hands.

21

COUNT YOUR BLESSINGS AND YOU WILL BE HAPPY

God, I am grateful today,
for all the things that money can't buy!
What would life be without eyes to see!
Wonder, without music, how happy could I be?

—AiR

People want to be happy, but somehow they end up living with stress and anxiety. Whenever I meet such people, I give them a simple remedy: if you want to be happy, count your blessings.

Instead, most people count their troubles. They keep listing all the things that are wrong in their life and they forget all the goodness that they are blessed with. I read a quote by Denis Waitley several years ago and it made me understand this truth: 'I had the blues because I had no shoes until upon the street I found a man who had no feet!'

We keep on complaining about what we don't have, instead of being grateful for what we have. Develop an attitude of gratitude.

COUNT YOUR BLESSINGS AND YOU WILL BE HAPPY

It will raise your altitude. I have made this the philosophy of my life. I make it a point to count my blessings, every day of my life. Even when there was trouble, I would count my blessings. This would make me grateful as I compared the positives I had with the negatives. The negatives are minuscule, but somehow people tend to focus on them.

What happens when we count our blessings? It gives us a sense of contentment and fulfilment and our life is filled with joy, bliss and peace. But some of us choose to live a disgruntled life, complaining and criticizing everyone, including God. It leads us to a life without faith, hope and enthusiasm, the very pillars of happiness.

When we count our blessings, we also bow down to the divine and thank the Lord for all the blessings. This makes us live with faith. What is FAITH? It is Full Assurance In The Heart. When we live with faith, we live with the belief that there is a power above that will create happiness in our life.

It also makes us live with hope. HOPE—Having Only Positive Expectations. When we bow down to the divine, we also believe and trust that divinity will make good things happen to us. Together, faith and hope become pillars, which help us bounce back, though we face tough trials and tribulations in life. Though we are made to face difficult situations, our faith, hope, belief and trust together help us overcome those bitter circumstances as we continue to count our blessings.

This leads us to live a life of enthusiasm. 'Entheos' comes from the Greek words 'in God'. When we trust or believe in God, we acknowledge that a divine universal power is in command and this creates a spirit of enthusiasm. It does not matter which religion we belong to, because all this is beyond religion. It is about having faith in the Creator as we count our blessings and live a life of gratitude, peace and bliss.

I have met many people who have not learned the art of counting their blessings. They do not live with faith and hope. They do not trust in a divine power. They have no enthusiasm. Their life is full of misery and pain. We human beings must acknowledge that there is a divine power that will grace us with peace and bliss. It is a belief in this power that makes us count our blessings as we live each day of our life.

TAKEAWAYS

- If you want to be happy, don't count your troubles.
- Develop an attitude of gratitude and it will raise your altitude.
- When we count our blessings, we live with faith, hope and enthusiasm.
- These are pillars that will help us bounce back in life.

22

CAN WE BE HAPPY ALL THE TIME?

*Why regret that I lived miserably yesterday?
Rather, why not commit and
resolve to live happily today?*

—AiR

About 2,500 years ago, there was a kingdom called Kapilavastu, ruled by Suddhodana. With great difficulty, his queen was blessed with a male child who was named Siddhartha Gautama. Siddhartha grew up in the lap of luxury. He was married to a beautiful princess and they gave birth to a lovely boy, Rahul. However, Siddhartha had a spiritual inclination. In fact, when he was born it was prophesied that he would become a great leader—either a great emperor or a great spiritual saint.

As Siddhartha grew up, he realized a profound truth—this world is full of suffering. He realized that no human being can escape from suffering. Whoever is born, must die and most of us experience old age and disease. Was there a way to overcome this suffering? Yes. One could live a life of bliss or nirvana. If a person is released from their attachment to desire and to cravings, they can attain nirvana. This is a state of liberation and freedom from suffering. This became the basis of his life transformation and he went to become the Buddha or the Awakened One.

The Buddha was enlightened with the truth that we cannot be happy all the time. The world is full of suffering and although he was a prince, he was forced to witness war, the mass killing of soldiers and several atrocities on the poor. What does the Buddha's life teach us? It teaches us that life is a mix of joy and sorrow. Just as we will be happy, there will be times when we will be unhappy, and we cannot escape this. However rich and famous we may be, we will grow old, may experience disease and decay, and ultimately, we will die. Even those who experience contentment and fulfilment cannot escape from the miseries of this world. Of course, the Buddha prescribed a way to nirvana, also known as moksha or enlightenment. But less than 0.0001 percent of the people in this world are fortunate to pursue this spiritual path.

The Buddha called his realizations the Four Noble Truths of Life. These are, dukkha—the world is full of suffering; samudaya—the origin of suffering is desire; nirodha—if we give up desire, we can escape suffering; and magga—the path to follow to renounce desires; this path ultimately came to be known as the Eightfold Path. The Buddha taught us that we cannot achieve nirvana unless we follow the Eightfold Path which refers to right understanding and intention, right speech and action, right livelihood and effort, right mindfulness and concentration. The Buddha described this path as a means to nirvana. Just like a raft is needed for crossing a river, it is by following this path, said the Buddha, that we can cross the river of samsara—the world—and be liberated from the cycle of death and rebirth.

CAN WE BE HAPPY ALL THE TIME?

In my journey of life, I was fortunate to learn about this truth that just as there would be happiness, I would also face unhappiness. Of course, since I evolved and moved out of living a life of pleasure, I was far more peaceful and blissful. But I still would experience misery and pain. With the help of my master, I went on a quest. I wanted to evolve to that ultimate state of happiness as experienced by the Buddha. Somehow, I believed that while we cannot be happy all the time, there was a way to realize how to transcend misery and suffering.

Not only did I study the life of the Buddha, but I also went on to study most of the religions of the world. My quest covered many profound questions but was ultimately aimed at discovering the ultimate secret of happiness. I had crossed the phase of pleasure that came from achievement, and I enjoyed tranquillity and peace that came from fulfilment. Now I wanted to be enlightened in a way that I could transcend misery and suffering. In my search for ultimate bliss and peace, I realized that we are none of these things—the body, the mind, the ego, but are the divine soul. The phrase, 'Neti Neti', from the Upanishads highlights this simple truth that we are not our physical body. We are the atman, the soul. How many of us truly understand the truth? Those who understand the truth realize the self and move on towards God-realization and the path of enlightenment. It was due to this profound realization that I was able to transcend suffering and live a life of bliss and peace.

TAKEAWAYS

- Just as we enjoy bliss, we have to face misery and sorrow.
- The Buddha realized that the world is full of suffering, but he also realized that there was a way to overcome suffering. It was called nirvana, moksha or enlightenment.

- In my search for ultimate peace, I realized that we are not the body or the mind or the ego but the divine soul. It was due to this profound realization that I was able to transcend all suffering and live a life of bliss and peace.
- The only way to be happy all the time is to evolve beyond the peaks of achievement and fulfilment to the peak of enlightenment.
- Enlightenment, nirvana or moksha is possible if we go on a quest and achieve self-realization.

23

THE PLEASURE–PAIN PRINCIPLE

Freud talked about the principle of pleasure,
The Buddha advocated the truth about pain.
The fact is that every human being wants to be happy,
and not live miserably in vain.

—AiR

Throughout life, we seem to be fitted with what I call a 'pleasure–pain' drive. Just like a machine has many drives, we are driven towards pleasure and are driven away from pain. What is this pleasure–pain principle?

Right from our childhood, there are things that give us pleasure like our favourite sport or our favourite food and there are things that give us pain. These could be burning our hand over a candle flame or pricking our finger with a pin. Because these experiences give us pain, we become cautious of a candle flame, needles and pins. This is nothing but the pleasure–pain principle in action. As we grow up, the principle doesn't change. Someone rightly said, 'The difference between the men and the boys is the cost of their toys.' We seek more expensive pleasures and we face bigger risks and challenges. However, we still seek happiness just as we shun unhappiness. This drive doesn't stop until our life ends. Even when we grow old, we still want things that will give us peace and bliss. It may be a sunset or a walk in the park. At the same time, we hate those things that cause stress and anxiety and try to avoid them. Though no two human beings in the world are the same, it is strange that all of humanity follows the same pleasure–pain principle.

Although it is very important to live in bliss and peace, it is equally important to find out what makes us miserable and eliminate that from our life. If we don't, then we are not following the pleasure–pain principle. What is crucially important in the pleasure–pain principle is that both these effects are directly connected. If there is happiness and bliss in our life, chances are that misery and sorrow don't surface much. But if we are suffering all the time, stressing and worrying, then the question of living with joy, bliss and peace does not arise.

Therefore, it is important for us to know what makes us happy and be happy, but it is equally important to know what makes us unhappy and eliminate such suffering from our life.

What is causing us pain today? A little virus that is causing cough and fever has torpedoed our life. It has affected our travel plans causing us much pain. Children are unable to go to school, just as we are unable to meet friends. As if from nowhere, a pain monster has arrived and stolen all our pleasures. Some people let their life become painful by living with fear. However, there are others who want to be happy. They take precautions, eliminate fear, wear a mask and go ahead with their task. Nothing is more important than their happiness. They find a way to overcome their pain. Isn't this the right way to live?

TAKEAWAYS

- We seem to be fitted with a pleasure–pain drive. We are driven towards pleasure just as we stay away from pain.
- Throughout our life, we repeat those actions that give us pleasure and resist those that give us pain.
- Since pleasure and pain together form a part of our happiness journey, it is as important to identify joy stealers as it is to identify happiness triggers.
- Once we know what are the things that make us unhappy, we must transcend them in order to live a life of joy, bliss and peace.
- We must be conscious of what is causing us pain and must eliminate the cause so that we can be in a state of bliss and joy.

24

IDENTIFY THE MESSENGERS OF MISERY

The messengers of misery will knock at your door,
worry, anger, fear, regret and more.
They rob your happiness and take your smile away,
if you let them enter, even for a day.

—AiR

Most often, our happiness is stolen by joy stealers like fear, worry, anxiety and anger. There are several such messengers of misery. They get this name because they bring bad news and carry with them misery, sorrow and unhappiness. The only difference is that these messengers carry not a message but misery. The most dangerous amongst these messengers of misery is fear.

Fear is not a real danger, but it creates stress. FEAR means False Expectations Appearing Real. Fear paralyses us and makes us suffer. We must eliminate this joy stealer if we want to be happy.

Another joy stealer is worry. Worry makes us anxious about the future. We worry about so many things like our health, our children,

IDENTIFY THE MESSENGERS OF MISERY

our financial condition and even silly things like the weather, a forthcoming movie plan or meeting our friends. We lose the present moment of joy by worrying about the future. Thus, we are advised, 'Kill worry before worry kills you!'

Natasha lived with fear and worry. She was a pessimist. She would not go for a walk because there was no sun, and she would not go for a walk because there was too much sun. Instead of finding ways to be happy, she found ways to be unhappy and went into depression. This is because she did not stop the joy stealers from being messengers of misery.

The next messenger of misery is regret, something that makes us live in the yesterday. Regret also steals our present moment. The only difference is that it pushes us into the past and by doing so, it steals our happiness.

Anxiety is another joy stealer. This messenger of misery makes us shuttle between the past and the future and guarantees that we become miserable. Instead of being happy in the now, we fall prey to anxiety, which robs our happiness.

The terrorist amongst joy stealers is anger. It creates a terror within that burns our peace and joy. While it tries to spit fire on others, it first burns our very heart. If we don't burn our anger, it will burn us.

One more amongst these messengers is doubt. Doubt is a silent killer! It tries to destroy our faith, just as it fills our life with hesitation.

Jealousy too steals our bliss and peace. This messenger often comes through the back door, quietly, without making its presence felt. It makes us envious of others' achievements and highlights our inadequacy, secretly pushing joy out of the front door.

Shame too can steal our happiness. It quietly eats into our self-esteem and makes us suffer. Just like shame, selfishness can make us unhappy because when we don't share with others, we are disliked, and we become distant and live miserably.

There are many more messengers of misery. Intolerance makes us snap at others, just as greed leads us to unhappiness. So does guilt. It goes deep within and makes us suffer silently. There is no need to feel guilty if we amend what we have done. But the messenger remains to make us suffer.

Another joy stealer is hate. Hate can make us truly unhappy. When we hate people, our job, our city or our food, it destroys our bliss.

What is a joy stealer? It is anything that steals our happiness—just like criticism. While it focuses on others' shortcomings, it robs our peace.

Revenge, too, can make us truly miserable. When somebody has wronged us, if we do not forgive them, we let misery enter our life.

There are several other joy stealers that together create depression. Slowly, but surely, they corrode our cheerfulness. One such joy stealer is the addiction to drugs and alcohol which may offer some relief in the moment, but may prove to be lethal in the long run. Robin Williams, the well-known and much-loved comedian, appeared to be happy and financially stable. But behind the public persona, he was battling an addiction to alcohol and drugs and struggling with depression, which can rob one of one's perspective on life. It impacts all aspects of one's life. Robin Williams was only sixty-three when he lost his battle with depression and committed suicide.

Ungratefulness can also be a powerful messenger of misery. If we do not live in gratitude, we will suffer. All these messengers of misery are powerful enough to steal our happiness. We must identify these joy stealers and eliminate them from our life. There may be many more such joy stealers. They are all enemies of happiness.

IDENTIFY THE MESSENGERS OF MISERY

TAKEAWAYS

- If we want to be happy, we must learn to eliminate joy stealers.
- These joy stealers act as messengers, but they bring misery and make us suffer.
- Fear, worry, hate, revenge and anger are some of the joy stealers.
- Whatever steals our joy is an enemy of our happiness. Beware! Do not let them enter your life.

25

TRIPLE SUFFERING KILLS OUR HAPPINESS

I—Want—Peace, I is ego,
Want is desire; remove ego and desire and you have peace.

—Sathya Sai Baba

Human beings experience what I call 'triple suffering'—suffering of the body, mind and ego. The body suffers through all kinds of physical pain. It may suffer due to an accident, or a physical disorder. As we advance in years, we are affected by diseases that cause pain. Even if we do not have any disease, every human being experiences a decay in their body before they die. Therefore, everybody experiences physical pain. This is our first suffering.

The second suffering is that of the mind. Worry, stress and anxiety are causing great suffering today to both the rich and the poor. As we become older, our mental suffering only keeps increasing.

Our ego suffers when it experiences the agony of disappointment and disgust. We get angry and upset. 'I told you to come here. How dare you disobey me?' screams the ego in agony. Every human being experiences the agony of the ego. And it is not just anger that is let loose when we allow our ego to get the better of us. Revenge, jealousy and hatred are all emotions that our ego can unleash.

Therefore, as we go through our life journey, it is natural to experience this triple suffering. How do we escape this? We can reduce our physical suffering by taking painkillers. Imagine doing a root canal without the dentist administering local anaesthesia!

But how can we reduce the suffering of the mind and the agony of the ego? There is only one way—we need to realize that we have a body, but we are not our body; we may have a mind, but we are not even our mind; and it is ignorance that causes us to believe that we are 'I'—the ego.

When we realize that we are not the body that we wear, but rather the ones who wear the body, then we distance ourselves from physical pain. When we watch our mind as somebody separated from the mind, we can slowly overcome mental misery. When we realize that we are the divine soul and not the ego that we appear to be, then we can escape the third suffering. Less than 1 per cent of this world goes on a quest in search of what is known as self-realization.

If we want ultimate bliss and peace, we must acknowledge this triple suffering. Different people evolve to different stages of realization and reduce the impact of the triple suffering. But there is hope that one can transcend the triple suffering entirely through realization of the truth.

There was a king who went to a spiritual master and told him that he was very stressed because he feared an attack from another king; his agitated mind did not let him sleep. The spiritual master told him to sit in silence for two hours in a room and focus on his mind. He promised the king that he would then remove all the stress and anxiety from his mind.

The king sat in silence for two hours, but he could not find his mind. There were all kinds of thoughts that continued to cause the king to worry, but he tried very hard to focus on what the saint had asked him to do—to find his mind. He could find his eyes, his head and his ears; he could even feel his heartbeat, but he could not find his mind! After three hours, the saint approached the king and said, 'I am waiting for you. I want to remove all the stress and worry from your mind.' The king replied, 'Where is the mind? I could not find it!' The saint then replied, 'How can you find the mind when it does not have any real existence? You only have bundles of thought that appear to be your mind. If you don't want stress and worry, then don't think those thoughts. Make a conscious effort and you will be free from stress and anxiety.'

The mind only appears to exist. I have seen X-rays and scans of my brain, my heart and of many organs, even of bones, muscles and nerves, but I have never seen an image of my mind.

My quest took me further to realize that I was not ME—Mind and Ego. When the body dies and the life energy within departs, I realized that the ME is reborn in a new body. My spiritual quest made me realize the truth—I am not even that ME. This helped me transcend the misery of my mind and the agony of my ego as I lived as the divine soul, the life energy within.

For the purpose of transcending the triple suffering, we need to go further on a spiritual quest. We need to know or, rather, realize that we are not our body, our mind or our ego. This will help us overcome the triple suffering and live a life of eternal bliss, peace and joy.

TAKEAWAYS

- Human beings experience triple suffering—the suffering of the body, the mind and the ego.
- The body suffers physical pain, the mind experiences misery and the ego, an agony of disgust.
- It is possible to overcome physical pain with medicine, but it is very difficult to overcome the misery of the mind and agony of the ego.
- We need to realize that we are not our body, mind or ego, but the divine soul. This will liberate us from the triple suffering.

26
OUR IGNORANCE MAKES US SUFFER

If ignorance is bliss, there should be more happy people.

—Victor Cousin

What is the primary cause of our suffering? If we truly want to be happy, we cannot ignore this important question. We suffer not just from physical pain, but also when we fall prey to our ego.

No doubt the body suffers. But we are ignorant; we are not the body. Although we say, 'this is *my* hand, *my* tooth, *my* head', we are impacted by physical pain and we believe that we are suffering. We do not understand that it is our body that is suffering, not us.

Let us take, for instance, a situation. Your car meets with an accident. It is damaged beyond recognition, but nothing has happened to you. Most people would get badly impacted even if they escape without a scratch. Still, they cry. The wise ones celebrate and say, 'My car had an accident, but I am perfectly okay.' Why should you suffer after such an accident?

OUR IGNORANCE MAKES US SUFFER

Once somebody asked me, 'Are you okay?' after I had just had a painful root canal. I replied, 'My tooth is aching, but I am perfectly okay.' I had already learned to distance myself from the physical pain of my body. But even if I have a severe headache, I learned to distance myself from the headache that *my* head was experiencing. Unless we overcome the ignorance that it is our body that is suffering, not us, we will continue to suffer physical pain.

What about the mind? When the mind worries and wanders, we become miserable. This is because we are unaware that we are not our mind. In fact, this lack of awareness is the source of all our suffering. Fear, worry, stress and anxiety are common mental ailments in the world today. Unless we overcome our ignorance, we will continue to experience the misery of the mind. In my quest, I realized that when I distanced myself from my mind, I found that my anxiety disappeared. It is not easy, but with constant practice, I learned to use my intellect to control my mind from its unnecessary rumbling that caused misery.

In the past, my mind would give me sleepless nights. It would take one miserable thought and replay it hundreds of times. It is just like a modern TV channel, which replays a horrific scene repeatedly from different angles to magnify it. The mind also brainwashes us into becoming miserable. Today, I do not permit my thoughts to go haywire. My intellect puts an instant end to the miserable thoughts as I live peacefully and blissfully. As long as I was ignorant, I too would suffer due to my miserable mind, which actually doesn't exist.

I must have experienced agony numerous times in life. My ego would keep saying 'this is *my* property', or 'that car is *mine*'. The 'I', 'my' and 'mine' of the ego agonized me as it created anger and frustration when my expectations were not met. I was ignorant of the truth that nothing is mine. The fact is that I was born with nothing and when I end this life journey, nothing will belong to me.

Then why does the ego cause so much agony? It is our ignorance that makes us suffer. I am grateful that my master guided me to overcome the 'triple suffering' that is caused by our ignorance.

As long as we are ignorant of the truth, we will continue to suffer, and we can never experience eternal bliss and everlasting peace. Hasn't the world lost its peace of mind today? Hasn't a little virus caused the world to stop? Although COVID-19 might not be as fatal as it is being projected to be, what is causing the panic to continue? It is our ignorance. Some countries have realized the truth and lifted the law of wearing masks in open spaces, but some continue to insist that they wear a mask even when walking down an empty street or driving alone in a car. People around the world have allowed ignorance to get the better of them and, thus, we continue to suffer. It is this very ignorance that stops us from self-realization and happiness.

TAKEAWAYS

- The primary cause of our suffering is our ignorance about the truth.
- We are ignorant about the fact that we are not our body, mind or ego.
- Because of this ignorance, we experience the triple suffering of physical pain, misery of the mind and the agony of the ego.
- If we want to experience eternal bliss and everlasting peace, we must overcome our ignorance and realize the truth.

27

THE ULTIMATE SECRET OF EVERLASTING BLISS, JOY AND PEACE

Ignorance makes us believe that the one who suffers is me.
Tears in the eyes and worry in the mind is what we often see.
When we realize that the one who cries is the body and mind, not me,
Then, from the Triple Suffering, we can be free!

—AiR

A seeker of happiness must first overcome the misconception that success is happiness. Having done so, the seeker must then move towards contentment and fulfilment. This will make him evolve from the happiness that is based on pleasure to the bliss that sprouts from being at peace. A seeker must do many things to evolve in the happiness journey. He must make a list of what makes him happy and pull on these happiness triggers at every opportunity. If we truly want to be happy, we must learn to be conscious of the 'now', live in the present and not swing between our past and our future. We must eliminate joy stealers that come as messengers of misery. Each of these secrets of happiness will help us evolve into living a much happier life. Some of us are even blessed to discover 'true' love that gives us bliss. All of this makes a genuine seeker of happiness live a life of bliss and peace.

While people enjoy a life of achievement, fulfilment and contentment, they are still unable to escape from the suffering of the body. Every human being experiences suffering that is caused by physical pain. Not only that, but we also experience the misery of the mind as it makes us live with fear, stress, worry and anxiety. However blissful we may be, have we not experienced the agony of the ego when we get disappointed and furious? Most of us cannot escape from the suffering of the body, the mind and the ego. To transcend this triple suffering, the seeker of happiness must overcome the ignorance that he is not his body, not his mind, not his ego. Once this is achieved, the ultimate secret of everlasting bliss, joy and peace is revealed to the seeker. The secret is, 'I am not this body, mind and ego that suffer. I am the divine soul.' Then there is no suffering, only seamless bliss. The fact is that every human being must suffer. Even though we overcome our ignorance, we still cannot kill our mind and our ego. We can transcend them, but as long as we are alive, the mind and ego will continue to make us suffer.

The first truth that we must realize is that we are not our body, our mind or our ego. This will liberate us from a lot of unnecessary suffering and make our journey of life blissful. In the Bhagavad Gita, verse 2.30, Lord Krishna tells Arjuna, 'O descendant of Bharata, he who dwells in the body is eternal and can never be slain. Therefore, you need not grieve for any creature.'

'I am not this body but a spirit—the soul' is an essential realization for anyone who wants to enter the spiritual world. Although we are not bodies and are pure consciousness, somehow we have become encased within the body. If we want ultimate

THE ULTIMATE SECRET OF EVERLASTING BLISS, JOY AND PEACE

happiness and want to transcend death, we have to remain in consciousness.

However, death is not the end. When someone dies, the mind and ego are reborn based on their past actions—karma. This means that we will suffer again. As the Buddha said, human beings suffer again and again until they are liberated from the cycle of death and rebirth, which is not an easy task. We need a bigger realization to be liberated from being reborn. Then we are united with the divine. There is no more suffering. This is our ultimate goal, to live as the divine soul.

When the body dies, one of two things happens. The mind and ego, along with karma, are reborn. If our karmic account is positive, we will be reborn in positive circumstances. If our karmic account is negative, then we will be reborn only to suffer the sins of our past. The law of karma makes no mistake, and none of us can escape from our actions. Realization of the ultimate secret of bliss, however, liberates us from this cycle of death and rebirth. If we realize the truth—that we are the divine soul, not the mind and ego—then the actions performed are not our actions. If we have no actions, then there is no karma and we are liberated from rebirth. To understand this, let's realize that we are the energy that gives life. A realized being knows that nothing belongs to him. Although he lives in the body, he knows that he is not the body. The body is only his habitat and an instrument to realize the truth.

We should live as observers, and free ourselves from creating karma. Our goal is to escape from this illusion and unite with the Creator when our life is over. If we follow this, then in death we are liberated from rebirth and are united with the divine. This blessing is rare, and a very small fraction of humanity is fortunate to experience this. This is because the mind and the ego stops us from such a realization, a realization that leads us to liberation and then ultimately unification.

How does one reach this ultimate realization? When we realize that we are not our body, we feel that we are our mind and our ego—both of which will be reborn. When we finally realize that we are not even our mind or our ego, then there is no rebirth. This happens because we are freed from karma. Karma belongs to the mind and ego. Everybody experiences karma from birth to death. But the mind and ego continue to experience karma in the afterlife as it appears in different bodies. When we realize that we are not our mind and our ego, then karma does not belong to us. This ultimate realization makes us drop all our karmic baggage like a bag of marbles in the ocean, to let it sink and disappear as we are liberated from the cycle of rebirth and are united with the divine to experience everlasting bliss, joy and peace. The realized being who sees divinity in one and all will not do bad karma. But we must remember that while we do good karma, we must not lay too much emphasis on the one who performs good karma for he/she is just the medium. Our karma should not be governed by our ego. This is the ultimate secret of happiness. We must do good karma only as an instrument of the Lord, acting on His behalf.

Can anybody live and escape from action?

No, we can't, but we can be free *in* action.

Whatever I do, the act is not mine,

I am thy instrument; the actions are thine.

As I progressed from one realization to the next, there was a war within. My mind and ego refused to accept that I was the divine soul. However, my realization, powered by divinity, strengthened my intellect to transcend my mind and ego. Every time the mind pushed me to believe that I was ME, my intellect shot down that thought with divine grace. Even today, while I believe that I am

THE ULTIMATE SECRET OF EVERLASTING BLISS, JOY AND PEACE

the happiest man in the world, I face an attack from my mind and ego, as it is provoked by the five senses of the body.

It is not an easy task to live as a realized soul, but it is the only way to transcend the triple suffering. Once we do so, we will be ultimately liberated from suffering that comes with rebirth and we will be united with the divine. This is the biggest challenge of our life.

How do I live as the happiest man in the world? As one who has realized the ultimate secret of joy, bliss and peace? I do so by living as the divine soul, not as a body–mind complex. I realize that I am only an instrument of the divine and my actions are not my actions. All this helps me live as a liberated soul, free from misery and suffering, enjoying bliss, joy and peace unknown to common men.

TAKEAWAYS

- We must discover the ultimate secret: I am not the body, mind, and ego. I am the divine soul.
- Not only must we overcome our ignorance to transcend the triple suffering, but we must also realize the ultimate truth and be liberated from the cycle of death and rebirth.
- When we realize that we are not our body or our mind or ego, but the divine soul, we realize that we are only an instrument of the divine. Then we see that our actions are not our actions and we are liberated from karma.
- This liberation after the ultimate realization leads to unification with the divine, which is the ultimate goal of life.

28

HAPPINESS IS LIKE YOUR SHADOW

If only you would turn your mind inward, in deep daily meditation, you would find the source of all true, lasting happiness existing right within the innermost silence of your own soul. Don't be like the musk deer and perish seeking false happiness in the wrong place.

—Paramhansa Yogananda

Have you ever noticed your shadow? If you walk towards your shadow, it goes further away. But if you stand still, your shadow remains. We don't realize the simple truth: happiness is like your shadow. The more we chase it, the further it goes away. Still, we relentlessly chase happiness. We seek success, achievement, money and fame to be happy.

Happiness, like our shadow, remains with us. But we are constantly chasing it. When will we learn to be still and to discover that happiness is within us? When will we stop looking for happiness in the wrong places?

HAPPINESS IS LIKE YOUR SHADOW

Once, I saw an old lady who was looking for her diamond nose ring that she had misplaced. Soon, many of her neighbours joined in the search. They asked her several questions. 'What are you looking for? Is it a real diamond? Is it cast in silver or gold?' They were all concerned and earnestly wanted to help her find her lost treasure.

Suddenly, one of them asked her, 'Do you know exactly where you dropped it?'

She replied, 'Of course, I am sure I've dropped it inside my house.'

'Then why are you searching for it outside?' he asked.

She replied, 'You don't understand. There is no light inside my house!'

Most of us are like this lady. We are searching for happiness, but we are not looking for it in the right place. How will we ever find it? First, we keep chasing success because we think success is happiness. Most people waste their life pursuing achievements but never get a sense of contentment and fulfilment. Is it not enough that we see the rich and famous live a life of misery and depression?

I am inspired by the story of a musk deer, an inhabitant of the Himalayas, who was frantically searching for the fragrance of the musk oozing out of its navel. The deer goes round in circles, looking for the source of the fragrance. Finally, it falls off the cliff and dies. When hunters tear open its navel, they retrieve the musk that was inside the deer all along. Unfortunately, it was ignorant—it did not know that what it was seeking was within itself.

We, too, are wanderers, much like the musk deer. We are not able to realize the truth about happiness—that it is within. We are searching for it outside, just like chasing our own shadow. When will we stop chasing this shadow of happiness and go within to realize the truth of who we are and why we are here? When we are still and when we contemplate the truth, only then will we open our *real* eyes and realize the truth. Life is not about chasing happiness; it is about *being* happy. To be happy, we must be still, aware and conscious of the truth. When we are conscious of the truth, then we will experience eternal joy and everlasting peace.

TAKEAWAYS

- Happiness is like your shadow. The more you chase it, the further away it goes.
- If we want to be happy, we must be still. Only then will we be able to experience true bliss.
- Just like the musk deer, we are not able to realize the truth about happiness, that it is within.
- We must not search for happiness in the wrong place. Happiness is within us.

PART C

HAPPINESS IS SUCCESS

Live before you die, what's the use of this race?
What will it get you even if you become an ace?
The purpose of life is to live with peace and happiness,
not just to run and, finally, die with a lot of success!

Happiness is success, success is not happiness.
Life is a journey that must be lived with peace and bliss.
Overcome the myth that you need success for happiness,
and realize the ultimate truth: happiness is success!

—AiR

29

THE HAPPINESS PARADOX

The paradox of happiness is you can't get happiness in a chase.
The more you go behind it, the more it hides its face.
We desire happiness, but we are unable to fulfil our thirst,
It is a sad paradox that feels like a curse.

—AiR

What is the happiness paradox? This paradox reveals that the more we chase happiness, the more elusive it becomes. In fact, the pursuit of happiness brings unhappiness.

For somebody hearing this for the first time, it may sound very confusing. How can seeking happiness lead to unhappiness? But for those who are fortunate to experience bliss, they realize that true happiness is a state of fulfilment, not achievement. This is because, despite achievement, there is no lasting happiness. Soon, we are looking for something else to make us happy. But when we reach a state of fulfilment built on a foundation of being fully content and satisfied, we experience everlasting happiness and peace.

You should not say 'I want to be happy'. This chase becomes the cause of unhappiness. You should just *be* happy. That is the secret of happiness. The moment you want to *be*, you create an expectation. The expectation may not be fulfilled and, thus, you may not *be* happy. But you can just 'be happy'. Nobody can stop you from being happy. It is a state of being. It is a choice. It is an attitude.

Over the years, I have met both happy and unhappy people. I have noticed that those who have everything often remain unhappy, whereas those who have very little are far happier. When I delved deeper, what did I find? The happy people chose to be happy despite their circumstances. But the ones who are constantly seeking happiness have conditioned their mind to be happy only if they achieve a goal or if they go to their dream destination or, further still, only if they experience moments with a loved one. The moment happiness becomes conditional, it escapes us. Even if a condition is fulfilled, we again create another condition to be happy. We must learn to be happy rather than become happy if a condition is fulfilled.

The happiness paradox is a very interesting concept and has thus become renowned globally. Researchers have analysed over the ages what people say makes them happy. Somebody says, 'I love to eat pizza, this is my moment of bliss.' But the moment they finish eating it, if you give them another pizza, the happiness quotient reduces. Somehow, they may eat it, but try giving them the thirdpizza. They hate the very sight of it!

When happiness depends on things, we tend to become less happy as we get more of the things we thought would make us happier. Our memories fade as we get used to the happiness resource, which, at first, felt so awesome. The paradox of happiness goes further to discover how the mind reacts to happiness. Apart from decreasing returns with the same product that we thought would make us happy, the mind also behaves weirdly when it comes to comparing our happiness with that of others instead of just being happy.

THE HAPPINESS PARADOX

A few researchers took video footage of the 1992 summer Olympics in Barcelona, Spain, to study the behavioural patterns of a few Olympic medallists during the award ceremonies. The gold medallist was very happy. The silver medallist was heartbroken because he missed the gold. But the one who got the bronze medal was jumping in joy because he didn't expect any medal at all! When we compare our happiness with that of others, we become unhappy. And further, when we don't expect to be happy, we become joyous. This is the happiness paradox.

Students at Yale University are said to have observed human behaviour along the lines of the happiness paradox. What did their case study reveal? Somebody works very hard to get into the best university. Very soon, they start feeling that this was no big deal. It was something that they aspired towards passionately, but in a matter of days, the achievement did not seem to create the happiness they thought it would. Similarly, people seek to make tonnes of money and after a lot of hard work, when they finally make it, they are dissatisfied. Either they want more or they don't know what to do with their hard-earned money. Or, worse still, they start living with the fear of losing their wealth. Several achievers who came under the spotlight of this study were seen to be bored and dissatisfied despite achieving their dream. So, happiness is not just about making our dreams come true. Happiness is all about being happy.

From the time we are born we are taught that success is happiness, but this is a fallacy. While most of the world continues to chase happiness to experience bliss, they will never experience true joy. Even if they are excited for the moment, they soon get on a new pursuit of happiness and no longer remain in that state of bliss and joy.

TAKEAWAYS

- The paradox of happiness reveals that the more you chase it, the more elusive it becomes.
- The pursuit of happiness can bring unhappiness.
- If we want to be happy, we must just *be* happy and not want to *be* happy.
- Things that make us happy slowly lose their ability to create excitement as we get more of it.
- When one's happiness is compared to that of others, even the happiest people become unhappy.

30

WHAT DO PEOPLE ASSUME HAPPINESS TO BE?

Happiness is just being blissful, not achieving success.
For success brings us pleasure, but also a lot of stress.
Miserable are those who zoom from womb to tomb,
gold and diamonds all around, but no peace in the room.

—AiR

We assume that the source of happiness is pleasure, wealth, money and success, when, in reality, happiness is something else. Every one of us wants to be happy, but somehow we don't seek true happiness. We just believe that success is happiness and from the time we take control of life till it's over, we seem to be in the pursuit of material success.

While it is perfectly acceptable that we must educate ourselves and try to be good at what we do, it is wrong for us to assume that all this will lead to happiness.

While money has a lot of positive uses and provides us with basic necessities, just as it promises us security and support for health, it is unable to buy true love. Love is a fountain of happiness. Haven't we heard hundreds of love stories where dozens of hearts were broken when a lover chose poverty rather than money as a choice from the heart? These are people who have chosen happiness over money and wealth.

Edward VIII, king of the United Kingdom, Northern Ireland and dominions of the British empire from 20 January 1936 to 10 December 1936, abdicated the throne to marry the love of his life—Wallis Simpson, who was twice divorced, and an ordinary American woman. He made this decision after the British government, the public and the Church of England condemned his decision to marry the American divorcee. He married Simpson and lived in exile till his death. The king obviously realized that happiness is not directly proportionate to wealth and power and thus sacrificed his royal life for a happy one.

The importance of money can never be misunderstood or underestimated, but to believe that money can buy happiness is a pity. The world has seen several examples of people who have committed suicide even though they were amongst the richest in the world. As the suicides of Kate Spade—an award-winning fashion designer—and Anthony Bourdain—a renowned American celebrity chef—clearly show, being successful doesn't make one immune to depression and suicide. If money could create happiness, why would the rich and famous end their life? Obviously, they were living a life of anxiety and misery and this led them to take such a drastic step.

Real happiness is a state of being happy. When we program our mind to believe that we will be happy when we go to New York, we miss the opportunity of being happy now. All these desires postpone our happiness to a tomorrow that doesn't exist. Dreams and wishes that are based on monetary pleasures are, in reality, joy stealers. Although they may fulfil the desires of our senses, they are self-gratifying and they will not create eternal peace and everlasting joy.

I know a lady who is crazy about handbags. Some years back, she bought a limited edition handbag of her favourite brand and it cost her a bomb. One day, her daughter was doing a craft project and she needed a patch to complete the project. Innocently, she cut a piece of the bag and pasted it on her craft work. When the woman saw her bag cut open, she was so upset that she hit her child—who had clearly not realized the value of the bag. This created so much stress for weeks!

Happiness is an art and we must develop this art of living in bliss. We cannot assume that things, people and places will give us happiness. When will we realize the importance of *peace*? When will we find true love? These are the real pillars of true happiness.

If you look around, everyone is trying to be rich and famous. They assume that this is the *only* way to happiness. People believe that once their desires are fulfilled they will be truly blissful. Kids are trying to get into the best universities and then be at a top position in a Fortune 500 company. Some are trying to start their own enterprises that can make them millionaires or billionaires. There are others who are trying to brand themselves in a particular way. Everybody is trying to be the best because there is no place for the ordinary. The world respects and salutes only the winners. But, stop and think for a moment—why should all this matter so much? Should we spend our entire life pursuing success when, in reality, we are seeking happiness out of that success? If there was a way to be happy without going through the ordeal of spending our entire life collecting achievements, should we not rather choose that? If in the final analysis all we want is happiness, then why should all this control our life, our actions, our priorities and our philosophy? I have spoken to many rich and so-called successful people, and I have mostly observed regret deep in their hearts. Many of them are regretful because they were so busy chasing success that it robbed them of their precious time and life. While the chase and the achievements are good for a short period of time, they cannot become our life itself; in the end, we have a lot of wealth created by success but no life left to be happy. And it's too late!

In this journey of life, there can be no freedom from action. We all have to do something with the aim to excel in our work. However, living a life being obsessed with making money, thinking that wealth is happiness, is foolish. True happiness is very different from monetary pleasures.

I, too, have lived with the constant expectation of success, which used to give me sleepless nights. In hindsight, my success was creating more stress than happiness. It was buying pleasures but not inner peace. It was getting me fame but silently stealing my bliss. It was no easy task to say goodbye to success, fame, power and position, but it would have been foolish not to do so.

This does not mean that money is the primary cause of unhappiness. But for those who think that *only* money can create happiness, this should be a wake-up call. There is no doubt that money can buy a lot of things, but it cannot buy happiness.

In the beginning, there was no wealth, although there was health and there was time. Then, we made wealth through success and there was health too, but there was no time. After a while, when we have created time to use our wealth to be happy, chances are that there will be no health to enjoy life. Now, it is time to wake up.

TAKEAWAYS

- Happiness belongs to the *now*, but our wealth imprisons us and promises us happiness in the future that doesn't exist.

WHAT DO PEOPLE ASSUME HAPPINESS TO BE?

- We assume that money can buy us things that make us happy, take us to places that give us bliss, but this is momentary.
- Money is important, but it is not everything. It is not a currency that can be exchanged to receive happiness.
- Money gives pleasure but doesn't give peace, the very foundation of our happiness.
- Finally, when we manage to make the time to use our wealth to be happy, we have no health because it's too late.

31

HAPPINESS IS NOT A DESTINATION

Stop! Take an exit now. Don't just chase success!
For you may find success, but you won't find happiness.
Remember the goal of life is to find peace and bliss.
But learn this simple truth, success is not happiness.

—AiR

Most people miss being happy because they think happiness is a destination. They want to *get* to happiness. They want to *become* happy. What they don't realize is that happiness is a journey, not a destination. We can be happy *now*. We don't have to wait to get happiness or to become happy.

What is life? It is a journey. Not a destination. The destination is death. Till we die, every moment is an opportunity to live in peace and bliss. But most of us have the picture wrong. We are busy constructing happiness for the future and losing precious moments in pursuit of a happy future.

While there are people who live to be a hundred, and while

our lifespan has marginally increased over time, the average life expectancy, according to the United Nations, is about seventy years. This means that each human being lives for about 25,000 days only. By the time we wake up to realize that our life is zooming by, we have probably consumed 10,000 days. What we don't realize is that we waste this valuable journey called life in pursuit of things that promise to make us happy in the future. Trading our present life for a possible future happy life is pointless.

It's really sad that many people spend their life without meaning or purpose. We just zoom through life without realizing that soon it will be over. Life doesn't come to us with a rewind button. The past is gone forever. But life itself comes to us one day at a time. Each day unfolds with twenty-four beautiful hours. Each hour has sixty valuable minutes and each moment clicks with sixty priceless seconds. Each moment of life is an opportunity to be happy, to live with peace and bliss. If we make the present full of joy, our life will be blissful. But we lose these moments in seeking a blissful future. Alas, we lose life itself.

I, too, lost many years of my life trying to create a future of my dreams. Before I could realize it, I was forty. I didn't even know how my youthful years zoomed by. They were all spent in pursuit of success. Now I hardly have 10,000 days to live, if I am lucky. I don't want to spend the next few years creating happiness for the future. I saw that many people had reached the end of their road hoping for a happy future. But they had lost out on life itself.

Suresh was a young man. He worked very hard to send his three children to school. It was a challenge to pay for their education and make ends meet. He was hoping that he would be happy once his children settled down. On his forty-ninth birthday, Suresh got a heart attack, and never woke up again. His entire life was a struggle for survival. It was a pity that he made happiness his last priority.

HAPPINESS IS SUCCESS

Many of us don't realize that happiness is not *a* priority, but *the* priority of our life. Whatever be the circumstances in our life, our ultimate goal is to live a life of peace and bliss, not just to enjoy success and pleasure but to achieve that ultimate state of eternal joy by discovering the true purpose of life.

When my mentor and master made me realize the truth that the journey of life was short, I started my quest to find the true purpose of life—at that time, I was forty-six years old. I spent two years in a retreat with the sole purpose of finding the ultimate truth of happiness. I am grateful that when I turned forty-eight, I realized the truth about life. I started living life meaningfully, peacefully and blissfully. For the past few years, each day of my life has been filled with bliss. Each moment of my life is peaceful as I am conscious of my real existence and enjoy divine bliss with every breath I take.

Those who want to achieve this state of eternal joy and everlasting peace must go on a quest. The time is now. There is no tomorrow. Nobody knows how long their journey of life will last.

Happiness comes from living blissfully, moment by moment. The destination is death. We must be happy every moment that we are alive.

TAKEAWAYS

- Most people miss being happy because they think that happiness is a destination.
- Life is a journey, not a destination. The destination is death.
- It is foolish to exchange our present moment of joy with a future that *may* make us happy.
- We must try to be happy every moment.
- Happy are those who enjoy the journey, instead of being preoccupied by the destination.

32

CAN WE CONTROL THE RESULTS OF OUR ACTIONS?

We can do our best, but are the results in our hand?
Results are controlled by someone whose
true power we don't understand.
We are just actors, we must do our part,
and the rest will unfold.
Whatever comes, just accept it;
live courageously with faith and be bold.

—AiR

A very important aspect of our happiness is understanding that the result of our actions is not in our hands. Most of us become unhappy when the results we expect do not turn out to be what we thought they would be.

An artist buys the best canvas. He pulls out his best paints and then sets out to create the painting of his life. Despite his best efforts, his painting does not achieve due credit. What is the cause, he wonders? A farmer buys the best seeds and does his best to plough the crop. Despite his best efforts, the crops fail. The farmer cries, but the results are not in his hands.

Man can do his best, but he cannot control the results of his action. This is what makes him unhappy. Man can perform certain actions with certain expectations, but he must realize that everything is not under his control. The results of his actions are influenced by several factors, such as other people's actions, market conditions, nature and forces beyond his control. But man doesn't accept this. When the expected results do not turn out the way he wants them to, he gets disappointed—he gets discouraged and feels defeated.

This universal truth led me to realize an important fact about happiness—we must not link our happiness to expectations. We should do our part and be happy for having done our best. If we expect something to happen and it doesn't happen, we create our own misery and unhappiness.

While we can control our actions, can anybody in this world control the results that will follow? I realized that man is in command of three factors: he is in command of himself, he is in command of the tools he uses, and he is in command of his efforts. Only these three factors are under man's control. However, there is a fourth factor that is responsible for the results of all our actions. This is beyond man's control. We often refer to this factor as a natural factor, a divine factor or a universal factor. We may give it any name, but it is this fourth factor that ultimately decides the results of our actions.

When I learned about this fourth factor, I realized how true it was. This is what makes somebody least expected to win, become Miss World in the beauty pageant. This is also what makes a sports star lose his championship title to the underdog. Big corporations fail when, suddenly, market conditions change and their products have no takers. Real estate tycoons collapse when a country introduces a law that makes them lose their competitive edge and they have no option left but to shut down their businesses.

I have seen hundreds of cases where the fourth factor was responsible for the results. You must be aware of a million-dollar company, Kodak, that used to make photo films. When digital photography was invented, Kodak had to shut down. Companies making audio and video compact disks lost millions when the trend changed. There are so many factors beyond the control of man that determine the results of his actions.

Since we cannot control the results of our actions, we must not set any expectations. The moment we create expectations, we have already sown the seeds of our misery. Today or tomorrow, we will face a situation that guarantees unhappiness.

How does this come in the way of success and happiness? We all want to succeed. We believe that when we succeed, we will be happy. This belief is based on expectations, but the result of our expectations is not in our control. How then can we assure happiness for ourselves?

As long as we link our happiness to expectations, there is no way that we can be happy. This is a recipe for unhappiness.

TAKEAWAYS

- Man is in command of three factors: himself, the tools he uses and his efforts.
- We think that success depends upon these three factors that are within our control, but there is a fourth factor that is beyond our control.
- Very often, it is the fourth factor which controls the results of our actions and, thus, our expectations are not fulfilled.
- Since we cannot control the results of our actions, we deliberately create unhappiness by expecting success, which is not in our control.

33

THE ART OF ACCEPTANCE

*The way to live with happiness is to live with acceptance,
not to desire and crave things and then face disappointments.
Whatever comes to our hands, just accept it with peace,
and enjoy every moment of life before your breath does cease.*

—AiR

If we want to master the art of happiness then we must learn to develop the art of acceptance. Happiness doesn't depend on what happens, but rather on how we react to what happens. If we learn to accept everything that happens positively, we can live a life of bliss and joy. We will become disgruntled if we expect rather than accept.

This is the major reason why success can never be happiness. Success is all about having desires and dreams and fulfilling them. However, many desires and dreams remain unfulfilled. Many a time, there are factors beyond our control that are responsible for results. We may do our best but the results may not always turn out as we expect. If we do not accept the results gracefully, we are bound to suffer.

THE ART OF ACCEPTANCE

My happiness grew from my learning to accept the divine will. For many years, I was so disappointed and unhappy. I would get discouraged when things didn't work out the way I thought they should. There were times when I felt so defeated; for example, I was fighting a case in the court and I was sure of winning but the judge pronounced the verdict against me. There were dozens of times that I was sure of success, but I faced defeat. This used to make me disgruntled. But I was a fighter, so I never gave up. I would fight with all my might to reverse the failures and usually I would succeed eventually, but this could never give me the happiness that I was seeking. It felt more like overcoming a hopeless struggle. The satisfaction, in the end, was more of a compromise.

Then, I slowly developed the art of acceptance. This made me live a life of bliss and peace. If things didn't work out the way I expected them to, I would still accept them gracefully. I would continue doing my best without any negativity poisoning my mind. This happened because I changed my attitude. Earlier, my priority was achieving success, but my priority soon became being happy. In the beginning, my ego would be hurt whenever things didn't happen my way, and I would become unhappy. Now, even though things do not happen the way I want, I gracefully accept whatever happens and retain my peace.

If we want to be blissful, then we must eliminate this passion for achieving success, which demands results and that things happen the way we like. But things don't happen the way we want them to happen all the time. If we want true happiness, we must not be attached to the results of our actions and become unhappy. We must accept whatever unfolds gracefully. The challenge is not to lose our inspiration but to do our best, knowing that is all that is in our control.

We are so goal-driven that we do everything thinking about

the results. For instance, we all work extra hours during our appraisal time, thinking that our bosses will rate us highly during our performance appraisal. This is something we need to avoid. If expectations are not met, pain is inevitable. Therefore, keep working and don't expect anything in return. Happiness, however, lies in learning to accept whatever happens thereafter. *'Karmanye vadhikaraste ma phaleshu kadachana'*—you have the right to work, but never to the fruit of work; this is the wisest message the Bhagavad Gita gives us.

We have a choice. We can live a life constantly chasing success, seeking the results of our choices and remaining unhappy, or we can do our best and let the natural will unfold, accepting whatever comes our way with peace and gratitude. What would you choose?

TAKEAWAYS

- If we truly want to be happy all the time, we must learn the art of acceptance.
- Happiness doesn't depend on what happens but rather on how we react to what happens.
- We must not be attached to the results of our actions and become unhappy.
- We must learn to do our best and accept whatever unfolds.

34

SURRENDER IS THE WAY

Surrender your life and then just live blissfully.
Learn the truth that whatever will be, will be.
For when we don't surrender, we lose our peace of mind;
though we achieve a lot of success, true bliss we'll never find.

—AiR

Apart from accepting the divine will, there is another important aspect of happiness. While acceptance has to do with whatever happens, surrender means we should hand over expectations to the divine will. Acceptance is just one part of happiness. When we accept, we don't regret. We learn to be happy, no matter what, but we keep hoping for good things to happen. We are constantly wishing for our dreams to come true.

Have you been to the Trevi Fountain in Rome? Thousands of people go there to drop a coin and make a wish. I was surprised when I visited Rome. You can see thousands of coins on the floor as tourists come to make a wish. It is said that those who make a wish at this fountain will have their wishes fulfilled.

Across the world, and not just in the Trevi Fountain, religions and cultures make people follow rituals and superstitions, which convinces people that their wishes can be fulfilled. What happens when we make a wish? One of two things happens: either it is fulfilled, or it is not. Therefore, those whose wishes are fulfilled believe in the prophecy and return again and again, giving such rituals and superstitions a longer lifespan. But what does this do to our happiness? When we wish for something and our wish is not fulfilled, we become unhappy. Some people are fortunate to master the art that overcomes this misery. It is the art of surrender.

Of course, working hard can make something happen, but can wishing for it make it come true? I do agree that the act of prayer, of bowing down to the divine power, can be an act that can fulfil our wishes. But just wishing is a powerless act. I have been a person who has lived with faith, hope, belief, trust and enthusiasm, and I know there is magic in an act of divine communication; I encourage people to do it. But having said that, we must also learn the art of surrender.

We must hand over what will be to the divine will. Yes, we should do our best, as much as possible. A meaningful prayer can help, but despite that things may not happen the way we wish.

I learned a beautiful prayer when I was young, one I often used to repeat.

When the idea is not right God says, 'No!'
When the time is not right God says, 'Slow!'
When we are not ready God says, 'Grow!'
But when everything is fine, God says, 'Go!'

Then, miracles happen, magic happens. The impossible becomes possible. We find a way where we thought there was no way. The divine has the power to create what we humans call miracles. But this only happens when we develop the art of surrender. I used to end the prayer with the line 'do your best and God will do the rest'.

We may belong to any religion, that hardly matters. God is a power beyond religion. It is this power that controls the universe through certain laws, just like the law of action and reaction commonly known as the law of karma. These laws are responsible for the ways things unfold. We are limited and we must surrender to the divine and accept the divine will.

What happens when we surrender? Our life is filled with peace and bliss. We are happy despite our wishes not coming true. We don't depend on success for our happiness. We develop the art of acceptance and surrender, and we are happier than most successful people.

I have lived my entire life with acceptance and surrender. I have experienced both the power of passion and the art of surrender, and there was a phase in my life when there was a fight between the two. I have learned that surrender and acceptance are far more powerful tools to make us happy than our passion for success.

Success may not make us happy, but I learned that when I accept and surrender, I am always peaceful and blissful. Having learned this art, I transformed my life and moved away from desiring and wishing to accepting and surrendering. I often chant a simple mantra: accept, don't wonder; replace hope with surrender. This filled my life with bliss.

TAKEAWAYS

- While acceptance has to do with whatever happens, surrender is to hand over expectations to the divine will.
- Success may give us happiness, but when we surrender, we live with peace and bliss.
- When we surrender and accept the divine will we are always happy.
- I have learned that surrender and acceptance are far more powerful tools to make us happy than our passion for success.

35

LIVE LIFE MOMENT BY MOMENT

*Those who are diseased with fear,
are sure to be deceased by it.*

—AiR

Franklin Roosevelt said, 'The only thing we have to fear, is fear itself.' The way to peace and happiness is to live life moment by moment, without letting fear destroy our treasure of the *now*. Today, our treasure has been hijacked by COVID-19 and we seem to be prisoners. Instead of living in the moment with peace, we are living in the future with fear.

Chanakya neeti says, 'As soon as fear appears near, attack and destroy it.' When our moment is attacked by COVID-19 and the consequences that may be, we should not submit to the myth that we will die of it. We should live with faith, knowing that death is in the hands of the divine.

Life is all about the present moment. Once it is over, then we must move to the next. If we want to be happy, we have to be happy now. Instead, if we let the fear of the virus destroy our present moment, then we will live in fear and lose our peace and happiness.

LIVE LIFE MOMENT BY MOMENT

I started writing this book in late 2019, and hoped to publish it in 2020. But COVID-19 ruined my plans. Everything was shut: the publishers and the printers, people were driven to work from home. Instead of living life moment by moment, everybody's moment was filled with sixty seconds of fear. While it seems like the virus originated in Wuhan, we did not spend a moment realizing that if it was actually a deadly virus, then there would be devastation in China. Country after country, survived the disaster of coronavirus, but in the bargain, we lost our valuable moments. Instead of living in the moment with precaution and peace, we let our moment be captured by the phobia of the pandemic. Some of us have recovered and taken control of our moments, but there are people who are still caught in the memories of those who have died and are paranoid about losing their own lives.

People who spent a moment investigating the truth were the intelligent ones who knew how to live with acceptance and surrender. They did not allow 'coronaphobia' and fear to dominate their life. They knew how to live life moment by moment.

What is the way to happiness? It is realizing that life is all about *this moment*. Once it is gone, it is over! Nobody can change the past, nor can we change the future. But we are in control of the present moment. We can choose to be happy or unhappy. We can choose to panic or take precautions. We can choose to live with fear or with faith. Not only are we blessed with an intellect, but we are also blessed with consciousness that can tame the monkey mind and stop it from continuing to yell and to yearn. What is this consciousness all about?

To be truly happy, we must live life moment by moment, in consciousness, not in thoughts. When we are bombarded by thoughts, then we lose consciousness of the moment. If we train ourselves to live with consciousness or awareness, then we make the mind still. We stop this bombardment of thoughts that otherwise steal our consciousness and our moments. To live with bliss, we must be conscious of every moment as it passes. We must not let thoughts of fear of COVID-19, thoughts of death and disaster, thoughts of destruction and pain, destroy our consciousness of bliss and peace. The choice is ours. We can live life moment by moment, or we can let a tsunami of thoughts destroy our moment and our life.

TAKEAWAYS

- To be happy, we must live life moment by moment.
- We must not let fear steal our moments. We must live with faith.
- Although there is a pandemic, we must use the moment to take precautions and not let the moment be filled with panic.
- We have a choice—we can live life moment by moment in consciousness, or let thoughts steal our moment and our peace.

36

MAKE HAPPINESS A HABIT

Make happiness a habit, don't let it be a 'some day' thing.
Live each day with bliss and peace, it is everything.
Learn to smile, be it sunshine or be there clouds that are grey.
Make it a habit that nobody can stop;
be happy every day!

—AiR

Everybody experiences moments of happiness and the whole world goes through the cycle of being happy and unhappy. But there is a way to be happy all the time. There is a way to be happy no matter what. How can we develop the habit of being happy all the time? The first principle of achieving eternal happiness is that it must not be dependent on anything. If our happiness is dependent on success, then our life will be spent caught in a yo-yo—being glad and sad periodically. To be truly happy we must transcend success and not make it the foundation of happiness. As long as our happiness depends on our achievements, we will become happy when we succeed and unhappy when we fail. Therefore, if life is latched on to success, you will never experience true bliss. You will think that life is very exciting, but deep within, there is misery.

How can one make happiness a habit? When we disconnect happiness from success, this is possible. If we learn to be happy, even without an achievement, we can experience bliss. When failure fails to steal our peace, then we have mastered the art of true happiness.

Recently, I met Nick and he spoke to me about life at length. He wasn't a happy man. He had too many problems. He was in a financial mess, and even his personal life created a lot of stress. In the end, I told him that a problem-free life is like an illusion. It doesn't exist. Everyone has problems. But just because you have problems, that is no reason to be unhappy. You can be happy despite your problems.

To experience true bliss, we must make it a habit. A habit is like a thick cable made of several wires. By itself, you can break a wire, but together, the cable is unbreakable. When we make happiness a habit, we remain happy, no matter what. No misery can break our state of happiness.

Over the years, I made happiness a habit. At first, my happiness too was dependent on my achievements until I took an exit and started living a life of contentment and fulfilment. I found that my happiness evolved and became dependent on peace rather than pleasure. I stopped when I reached my need and eliminated my greed, and I chose to be happy no matter what. All these are the basic requirements to make happiness a habit. To add to this, I used my intellect to control my mind. I stopped joy stealers from ruining my happiness and constantly pulled on happiness triggers. I did those things that made me happy as often as I could. I made it a habit to make others happy and I counted my blessings. And this eliminated whatever gloom I had in my life.

I also learned to live a life of acceptance and divine surrender. It's not that my life had no problems, but I realized that in the end, nothing matters. So, why be unhappy? I shut the door on my past and refused to let my mind go there to rehearse a regret, just as I tied down my monkey mind from jumping into the future and living with fear or anxiety. All this together became the secret recipe for happiness. This was a simple way to master the art of eternal bliss, and I made it a habit to be happy all the time.

If you want to be truly happy, then master the art of happiness and make this habit a part of your life. Don't let the messengers of misery knock at your door, no matter what. Don't let success and achievement control your happiness. Choose to evolve to a life of fulfilment, find the true meaning and purpose of your life. This will help you to overcome ignorance and liberate you from the triple suffering.

While it is possible to make happiness a habit and experience eternal bliss and everlasting peace, it is not everybody's cup of tea. It can be achieved by conquering your biggest enemy—your mind. If you resolve to be happy, nothing in this world can stop you.

Remember, things may happen to you and things may happen around you. But happiness is about all that happens within you and that is within your control. Choose to make happiness a habit and experience the bliss you have always desired.

TAKEAWAYS

- You can be happy no matter what, if you make happiness a habit.
- To make happiness a habit, make a conscious choice to be happy.
- Don't swing from the regrets of yesterday to the fears of tomorrow.
- The happiness habit is like a thick cable. Nobody can break it.

37

WE ARE HUMAN BEINGS, NOT HUMAN DOINGS

Realize! We are human beings; we are not 'human doings'.
Don't just do and do, like puppets on strings.
Be a human being, be conscious of the now.
Don't lose this precious life, just grazing like a cow.

—AiR

Why are we human beings? It is in the *being* that happiness exists. Not in the *doing*. When we are in a state of being, we become conscious of peace and bliss that is within us. We experience true happiness. But instead of living as human beings, we have become 'human doings'. All through life, we keep doing things. We strive for success because it promises happiness. Success makes us do things, but in the process of achieving it, we lose consciousness, which is important for attaining eternal bliss. Success will only give us momentary pleasure that will dissolve in a moment.

True happiness is being conscious of who we are and why we are here. Most of humanity does not experience this consciousness of being human. This is because we are so busy doing things.

Sages over the centuries have prescribed a simple method to be happy. They say that we must spend time in silence every day, even if it is for a few minutes, and preferably at the same time every day. Why have they prescribed silence as a means to happiness? This is because it is during these moments of silence that we are able to be conscious and experience bliss. Silence cultivates the being that we truly are, the divine soul. It is for this very reason that meditation, yoga and the like have gained popularity in the world. However, very few people understand the true meaning and benefits of meditation. It is not a just a stylish lifestyle choice for well-being, but a path to discovering the essence of truly being divine.

We are becoming busier by the day. Modern technology and the gadgets that are being created have stolen the silence we had and enjoyed. People have no time for self-discovery and for experiencing what it is like to be a human being because we are disoriented by the virtual world. We are constantly doing things, and most of our free time is spent on a laptop or mobile phone. We don't realize this, but the more we are 'human doings' rather than 'human beings', we are losing the opportunity of being blissful and peaceful.

In the pursuit of being well connected with the world, and achieving so many things, we have lost the art of being happy. When I discovered the importance of being conscious of who I was and my life purpose, I experienced a new state of bliss, one I had never experienced before. Not only was I living a life of fulfilment, but my conscious being also eliminated all misery and suffering that was always present when I was constantly chasing success.

I stopped living as a 'human doing' as I realized I was a human being. Although there was no freedom from action, I learned to enjoy freedom *in* action. I lived consciously and experienced eternal joy and everlasting peace. Some call it ananda, and some nirvana. To me, it was a state of *satchitananda*—a state of ananda (bliss) from the consciousness (chit) of truth (sat). *Sat–chit–ananda* is a Sanskrit term that describes the nature of reality as it is conceptualized in ancient Hindu and yogic philosophy. A common translation of *sat–chit–ananda* is truth–consciousness–bliss. This was probably one of my greatest realizations about eternal happiness.

We all have a choice. We can continue to be human doings or be the human beings that we are meant to be. We can either chase success or stop and enjoy moments of blissful silence by being conscious of the happiness that is within us. Once we realize that happiness lies within us, we will stop chasing happiness and learn the art of just being happy.

TAKEAWAYS

- We are human beings but we have become 'human doings'. All through life we are just doing things.
- Because we are in pursuit of success, we fail to live like a human being, experiencing who we truly are.
- Divine bliss lies within us, but we are unable to be conscious of this because of our constant activity.
- One way to be a human being is to spend more time in silence and experience bliss.
- Eternal bliss is experienced by one who lives in a state of *satchitananda*—the bliss that comes from the consciousness of the truth.

38

IN THE END, WE WILL HAVE SUCCESS, BUT NO TIME

Life is like a glass, it's full of time,
we spend our time, trying to make a dime.
Soon, we find, there's no time—just a lot of success,
we have so much money but no happiness.

—AiR

If we look at a typical person's life, we notice that one begins one's life journey with a lot of time. Slowly we trade our time for success. We spend our entire life trying to be successful. Some of us are fortunate and we become successful, but it is most unfortunate that we are left with no time.

A successful person spends his entire life achieving and chasing success. Because he thinks that success will give happiness, he postpones his happiness for the future and focuses on accumulating success. Before he can realize it, his life is over. He forgets to spend his life joyously doing the things he truly loves.

Success creates a passion, an obsession in the achiever. The world is like a stage on which the drama called life is enacted. We are like actors. We come and we go, but we don't realize that this is just a show. Somehow, we believe that we are going to be here forever and start building properties, establishments, relationships that do not last forever. Eventually, the show will be over and nothing will belong to us. Our pursuit of success doesn't make us realize this truth.

Instead of enjoying this journey called life, sipping it like an exotic drink, moment by moment, we rush through life, chasing success that we will ultimately leave behind. It is ironic that intelligent people have time to achieve all the success in the world but no time to realize this truth.

Chasing success is like flogging a dead horse. Success promises us an amazing future, but unfortunately, there is no guarantee of such a future. If you stop and look around, you will find successful people who enjoy their success but forget to enjoy life. They may have a great lifestyle and may seem happy on the outside, but deep within, their life lacks blissful peace and joy that is essential for true happiness. The rich and the famous are intelligent people. Their success is proof of this. They make a lot of money, but eventually it is their ignorance that lets them trade their success for their life.

On the other side, I see people who are not successful yearning to be successful because it appears to them that successful people are so happy. These onlookers, too, miss the bus when it comes to enjoying life that is a gift to them. Instead of counting their blessings, they are enamoured by the glamour of success, and in pursuit of the desire to be successful, their life escapes them. They too miss living a life of peace and joy.

TAKEAWAYS

- The idea of success drives us to achieve more, but in the bargain we lose out on life itself.
- Of what use is it to have more money, more property and more material things and have no life left?
- The rich and the famous are intelligent people. Their success is proof of this. But when it comes to living a life of peace and bliss, they are ignorant and have not realized the truth.
- Life on earth is like a humongous cosmic drama. We come and we go. When will we realize this is just a show?

39

LIVE BEFORE YOU DIE

There are many in this world who exist; they don't truly live.
They earn and earn and, finally, die; little do they give.
If you want to truly live this beautiful gift on earth,
then learn to live before you die or you will just take rebirth.

—AiR

What is the purpose of our life? Most people do everything else but have no time to ponder over this. We are born and before we know it, we become adults and are faced with life. What is life? It is the journey between birth and death. Whatever part of our life is over—it is finished. We can do nothing to change it. You can go to New York and London but you cannot go to yesterday, last week or last year. Such is life. The past is gone forever, never to return. Still, many people live in the past. They are constantly thinking about what happened and by doing so, they lose out on their present moments of life.

Some people don't look back. They realize, 'If the past is what they were meant to see, then behind, not in front, their eyes would be.' They look forward; however, they look so far ahead that they forget to live in the present moment. They are constantly losing today for a tomorrow that never comes. Very few people are truly living their life—moment by moment, each day in peace and bliss.

Although many know that life is a journey and not a destination, they let the journey escape and lose the beauty of the gift of life. There are many who are busy adding years to their life, instead of adding life to their years. Of what use is it if we have a longer life but not a happier one? What matters is not whether we live till we are fifty, sixty or seventy, but how we live! Even ten years of our life that are full of peace and bliss is far better than fifty years that we drag through with misery. Unfortunately, most people forget to live before they die.

Live before you die! Death is certain. Nobody can escape it, but we have an opportunity to live blissfully and joyously. Most people get so carried away that they pursue pleasure and end their life battling for peace. They struggle with their success, but lose life itself.

Everybody wants to be happy, but not everybody is. Most people think that happiness depends on what you have. But in reality, happiness depends on how you live. Very few people realize that peace is the foundation of happiness. It is far more important than momentary pleasure. These are the ones who live a happier life. They live a life of contentment and fulfilment and don't spend their entire life pursuing achievement. At least these people live life before they die.

But who are the ones who truly live life? They are not the ones that transcend greed and live fulfilling each need. A very few among us are lucky to truly live life. These are the ones who go on a quest to understand the true meaning of life. They don't live like a piece of furniture that exists in one place till it is moved away. They live a life of meaning and purpose. They try to find out who they truly are and why they are here. They go in search of the true meaning of life and if they are fortunate, they discover a life that is devoid of suffering and pain.

In the quest to learn what life is all about, they realize that the body will suffer and die, but they are not the body. The body is something that they wear. They also realize that the mind causes misery, just as the ego experiences agony. They realize they are not the ME—Mind and Ego. They realize that they are the divine energy that is life itself. Such realization liberates them from all kinds of misery and suffering. They are the ones who truly live life.

To truly live a life of bliss and peace, one must realize the truth about life. This is not a game for the ordinary. Only a few people are lucky to pursue the truth. These people are the ones who truly live before they die.

TAKEAWAYS

- Life is a journey between birth and death. Death is certain; nobody can escape it.
- Most of us just exist. We seek pleasure and ultimately die.
- Less than 1 per cent of humanity realize the truth about life, knowing that they are not the body. They are not even ME—the Mind and the Ego. They are divine energy.
- To truly live a life of bliss and peace, one must realize the truth about life.

40
SUCCESS IS NOT HAPPINESS, HAPPINESS IS SUCCESS

Success is not happiness, happiness is success.
Unfortunately, we have not been taught what life truly is.
We spend our life trying to be an ace in the race,
our life gets over and we are caught in the maze.

—AiR

While the whole world is in the quest to find these two treasures—success and happiness—we have not realized a simple truth. We want success because we *think* that success gives us happiness. If success were to make us miserable, would we still want it? Therefore, the world must come to terms that there is only one thing a human being actually wants—happiness! We must be absolutely clear that the purpose of life is to achieve true happiness—happiness that is built on a foundation of peace.

Success is not happiness—this is a myth that must be busted. As long as we believe that success will give us happiness, we can never enjoy true bliss and peace. We know the difference between pleasure and peace, between momentary happiness that comes from success and everlasting peace and eternal bliss that comes from true happiness. Still, most of us chase success for happiness.

As long as we believe success is happiness, we will never experience true happiness. We may achieve all the glory in the world, have unlimited financial resources, live in expensive villas, drive high-speed cars, eat exotic food and travel to every possible destination. Still, we will not experience true happiness because success is not happiness.

Success is success. It can give pleasure, but it cannot give true happiness. Our objective in achieving success is to experience true happiness. But ultimately, we only achieve success. True happiness eludes us.

Success is not happiness. Happiness is success. I realized that we are all chasing success because we want happiness. Although we are achieving, we are not happy. But if we can be happy, then there is no need for success. Therefore, I realized a profound truth—happiness is success.

Robert was a multi-millionaire. He had made millions, using which he bought several homes, offices, yachts and lived a successful life. He firmly believed that success is happiness. One day, he was walking along the pier and saw a fisherman on one of his boats playing with some kids. The fisherman was his employee named Tom.

'Hey Tom,' he said, 'what are you doing? Why don't you go and catch some more fish?'

Tom replied, 'I have caught enough fish for the day.'

Robert said, 'Why don't you catch more fish and make more money?'

'What would I do with more money?' replied Tom.

'Oh, you could buy a boat and appoint some fishermen and slowly buy another boat.'

Tom replied, 'What will I do with boats?'

The millionaire replied, 'Then you can be rich—like me.'

Tom responded with a puzzled look, 'Why would I want to do that?'

'Don't you understand?' Robert said. 'Once you buy boats and you become rich like me, you can truly enjoy life and have fun.'

Tom replied, 'But, Sir, what do you think I am doing right now?'

What successful people don't realize is that they don't have to be successful to be happy. Thus, they continue living their life pursuing success. I realized that the truly happy people are the ones who are truly successful. They are the ones who live life blissfully, without madly running after success.

Happiness is success! When I realized this truth, I gave up my success to experience true bliss and peace. I spent years living with contentment and fulfilment as the happiest man in the world. It was then that I learned the ultimate secret of how to be liberated from misery and sorrow. Since then, I have lived a life of eternal joy and everlasting peace, trying to help people discover the truth about life, trying to make people realize that success is not happiness, happiness is success.

TAKEAWAYS

- Success is not happiness because it can only bring momentary pleasure.
- Still, we all chase success because we think success is happiness.
- In reality, happiness is success because it achieves the objective of success—to be happy.
- Because we don't realize the truth, we continue to pursue success even though we really want happiness.
- If we are truly happy then we have already achieved success.

41
CHOOSE TO BE HAPPY, NOT SUCCESSFUL

'I'll be happy, not successful,' this is said by those who are wise.
I want peace of mind and not wealth that multiplies.
Life is meant to be happy and our purpose, we must find,
then we are liberated from the misery of ego, body and mind.

—AiR

What are you truly seeking? Do you want to achieve a lot of success and live a life of stress and anxiety, or do you want to live a life that is filled with peace and joy? You have a choice. Like everybody else, you too can believe the myth that success is happiness and live your life trying to be successful or you can live a life that's full of peace and bliss, living each moment with happiness.

It's time to realize the truth. Success and happiness are two different things. If we choose success, we can never experience true happiness, but if we choose true happiness, then this is the biggest success of our life.

CHOOSE TO BE HAPPY, NOT SUCCESSFUL

Man's greatest realization is this—happiness is success. Because man lives in ignorance, man thinks the reverse to be true—success is happiness. This can destroy our entire life and deprive us of our ultimate goal—happiness.

You may be shocked to hear this but, by and large, it seems to be true—success is not happiness; in fact, it is the enemy of happiness. When we chase success or achieve success, we are actually sacrificing our peace and tranquillity. In reality, there is nothing wrong with success, provided our focus is on happiness. We should not lose ourselves in chasing success. Our focus is to live peacefully and blissfully without craving success.

I made the choice to be happy, not successful. What did I do? I achieved enough success. I escaped from that maze which led me from one success to another. I got out of that mad chase that made me desire more and more. And I started living a life of pure bliss and peace. Earlier, my focus was on being successful. There was so much stress and anxiety. Now, my focus is on being blissful. I am so peaceful.

I looked around at the happiest people in the world. And I realized a divine truth. Many of them were yogis and sanyasis. A yogi is one who lives in divine union experiencing enchanting bliss all the time. He sees everything as a manifestation of the divine and lives consciously in ananda. A sanyasi is one who has renounced success and material pleasure. A true sanyasi lives a normal life and enjoys all that a normal man does, but he does not crave or desire anything. Whatever comes his way, he accepts it as a blessing from the divine and enjoys it.

Genuine yogis and sanyasis live a life of bliss and peace. They are happier than the millionaires and billionaires of the world. They endorse the truth—happiness is success. Every human being has a choice—to be happy or to be successful. Most of us want both, but what we don't realize is that our pursuit of success steals our happiness. Instead of living a life chasing achievements, we should spend our life seeking enlightenment or the truth. Enlightenment will eradicate ignorance, which makes us miserable. It will help us realize the truth about life, and live with tranquillity and joy.

So, man's ultimate goal should be enlightenment. For it is this state of being that blesses a man to live blissfully without any anxiety. When a man is enlightened, he discovers the purpose of life. He realizes who he truly is. And this opens the door to eternal happiness. The moment a man is enlightened with the truth, he is liberated from all suffering and misery experienced by an ignorant man. He becomes conscious of his true reality and lives in that divine consciousness blissfully and peacefully till his last breath.

Instead of achieving this true treasure of enlightenment, most of us are chasing a shallow goal of achievement and, soon, our life is over. We may achieve success, but we may never achieve true happiness. When will we discover the ultimate secret of happiness? When will we make the conscious choice to be happy—not just to be successful?

The time is now!

TAKEAWAYS

- We have a choice—to be happy or to keep chasing success.
- Most of us want both, but we don't realize that happiness steals success.
- The truly successful ones live a blissful life renouncing success. They are blessed to be enlightened and to realize the truth.

CHOOSE TO BE HAPPY, NOT SUCCESSFUL

- Realization of the truth not only enlightens them but also liberates them from misery and suffering.
- Instead of seeking something shallow like achievement, they achieve the purpose of life through enlightenment.
- They are the ones who are truly successful for they have chosen happiness over success.

AFTERWORD

MY 'GIVING' JOURNEY

I had nothing, but whatever I got,
I started to give.
The more I gave, the more I got!
What a magical way to live!

No doubt the world saw me as a successful person because whatever I touched turned to gold. There was success and more success. But the world did not understand the secret of my success. To me, the secret was simple. It was based on the universal law of Karma: *'As you sow, so shall you reap.'*

Whatever I made from my first success, I gave a lot of it away. Somehow, I did not have the habit of being selfish, or hoarding and storing my wealth. I don't even know why I kept giving, because it started when I was a child. Today, I feel grateful that I was blessed to give, for I realize that it is in giving that we receive. One thing is sure, my success was fuelled by my giving. The deeds of charity and service undoubtedly became the seeds that created the roots of success, the shoots of prosperity and the fruits of wealth and happiness.

I gave as much as I could to everybody, not just my family and friends but strangers as well. I would give my love to old people

AFTERWORD

who needed help while crossing the street. I would share my meals with those who worked in our household. When I started earning, I shared my income with the poor and the underprivileged who were sleeping on the streets. What I am sharing is not some theory. It is my personal experience that the more I gave, the more I received. In fact, I received much more than what I gave away.

My giving continued as my success hit the skies. I made millions, but I also gave away millions. It had become an automatic circle of my life. I experienced great joy in giving and this inspired me to give more and more.

From my initial business success, I set up a humanitarian trust. Our goal was to pick up people from the street and put them back on their feet. Some people had not eaten for days. They would have died. It was through divine intervention that the team in our trust, which was full of people with compassion and humanitarian hearts, was led to serve the destitute and the downtrodden. We found beggars on the street, and we set up small shops for them and provided them with merchandise to sell so that they did not have to beg for a living. When houses were ravaged by rains, we would reconstruct the roofs of the houses of the poor. We did anything and everything possible to serve the needy.

I was barely 30 when I started a weekly 'Giving day'. Every Monday, I would sit and wait for people to come to me with their problems and needs. I would personally listen to their stories and try to find a way to help them. We helped thousands of people live with dignity and respect. We gave medicines to the poor, just as we funded their surgeries and treatment.

As we did this, we realized that the existing charitable homes had limitations. They had too many conditions for admission and did not admit everyone who needed support. We found a child who was both mentally and physically challenged. Since we supported and sponsored several charitable institutions, we approached them for admission. One of the institutions said that they could only take care of the physically challenged, while another institution stated that they could take care of only those who were mentally challenged. We were left helpless and hopeless.

We decided to set up our own humanitarian home. We bought a piece of land and constructed a 100-bed home. We had a few cases that could not find admission in any charitable institution. A poor maidservant had a child, and she approached a charitable orphanage. They refused to accept the child unless she promised to never see her child again. Sobbing and crying, she brought the child to us. Hundreds of such cases, of people who are turned away at charitable homes, still come to us. We admit them in one of our three charitable homes. Currently, we have about 700 people staying with us. We look after them providing food, clothing, medicines and our love and care. They are our family!

Where did the money come from? I don't even know. All I know is that when we wanted the money, it was always there. There was never a time when we were short of funds. Even today, we spend millions to serve the poor, and while there are several supporters and donors who contribute to this mammoth but humble effort, it was 'giving', for sure, that led to us receiving the funds and support we needed to make all this possible. While I gave a lot to the destitute, I also wanted to do something for God. At that time, I was deeply religious, and my faith made me build a 65-foot tall statue of Lord Shiva. Little did I realize that in trying to give, by building a temple for my God, I would get another source to do bigger charitable projects.

The 'giving' journey has never stopped since then. I have evolved from a religious to a spiritual person, and my transformation has led to my metamorphosis. I continue to lead the charitable and

AFTERWORD

other organizations that I have set up. But personally, what I now give to others are my realizations. I give away books, just as I give away a lot of innovative merchandise that can help people realize the truth about life. While I can't 'give' enlightenment, I can give talks and provide answers to questions that can help people on the ultimate journey of self-realization, enlightenment, liberation and unification with the divine. This is the mission of my life. If I reflect upon my life, I am grateful for all the blessings that I have received. I realize that in the beginning, it was the law of karma that was working. But I went beyond doing good karma to becoming a karma yogi. I realized that every creature—be it a human being or a beast—is nothing but a manifestation of the divine. I experience God as SIP, or the Supreme Immortal Power in one and all, and so, I serve not the body that is suffering, but the temple that houses the soul that is none other than the Supreme Immortal Power. This has transformed me into a karma yogi, or the one who is ever-united with the divine through acts of good deeds or karma.

Right from the beginning, I knew that nothing is mine, that we come empty-handed and we leave empty-handed. I was blessed to live with detachment and even today, I try to give away as much as I can. I even realize that it is not me who is giving, these hands are not mine. I am just an instrument of the divine. It is the divine will that causes the 'giving' through my hands. It may appear that I give, but in reality, all 'giving' is that of the divine. If only we realize this and learn to live and give, we can not only enjoy the blessings of the Supreme Immortal Power that will liberate us from the triple suffering on earth—pain of the body, misery of the mind and agony of the ego—but also be united with the divine ultimately, as we are liberated from the cycle of rebirth.

We may pray to a God, but we do not realize that God is

not God. God is the Supreme Immortal Power, residing in you and me. We are ignorant about this truth and thus refrain from giving while living. If only we realize that we are nothing, and that we are all part of that one Supreme Immortal Power, we would give everything away. Somehow, the body, mind and ego, keep us trapped in ignorance and we do not realize that we come with nothing, and we will go with nothing. The ego makes us believe that I am 'I' and this is mine. I was lucky to realize that nothing is mine. Everything is Thine! Even I am Thine, O Divine! With this divine revelation, my life has evolved to where it is today. I hope that I continue to give as I live and when that day comes when it is time to go and I hear the death whistle blow, I should have given away everything that I have. I aspire to give before I am gone so that I become one with the divine and I am not reborn.

When it is time to go and I hear the death whistle blow,
May I have given away all that seemed to be mine,
This is my prayer, O Divine!

AFTERWORD

'IF WE DON'T GIVE, WE DON'T LIVE.'—AiR

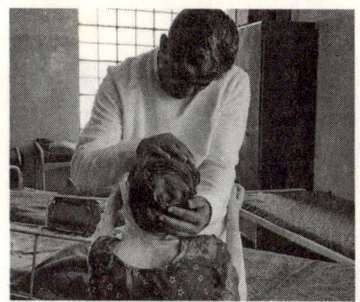
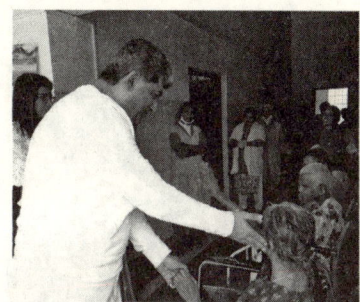

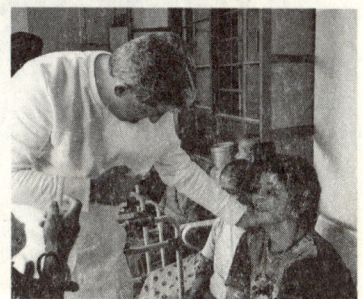

HAPPINESS IS SUCCESS

TO AiR, SERVICE TO HUMANITY IS PRAYER TO GOD.

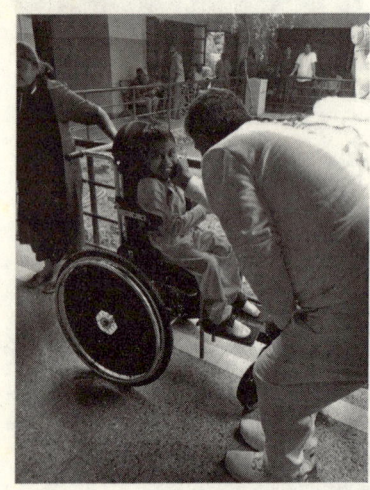
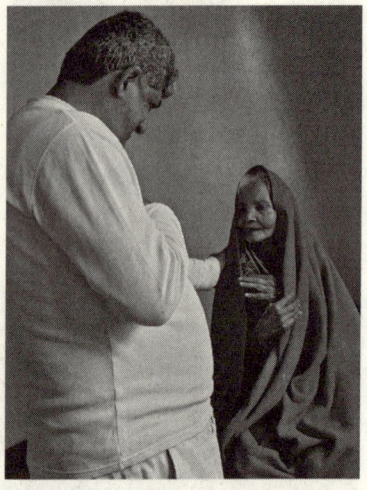
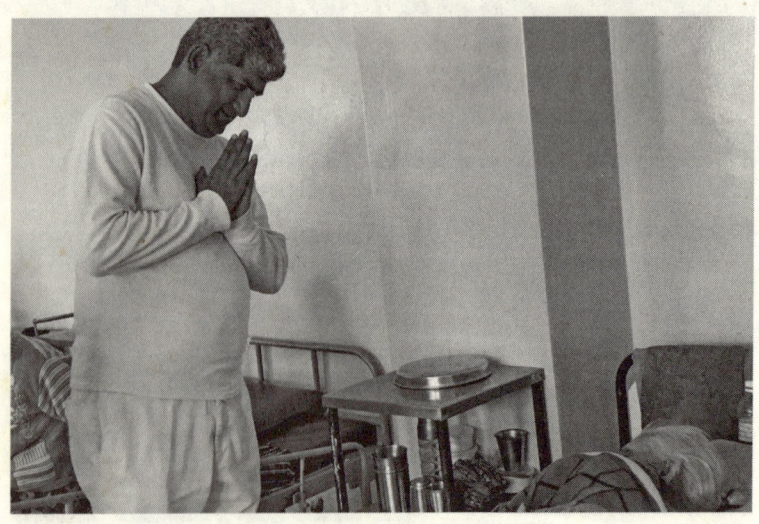

AFTERWORD

'WHEN WE LOVE THE POOR, THE DESTITUTE, WE ARE LOVING GOD.'—AiR

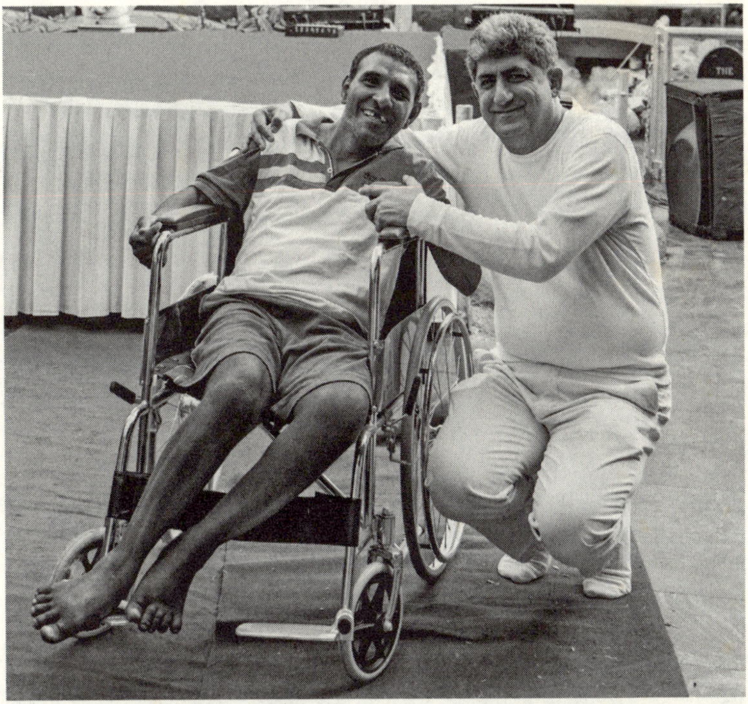

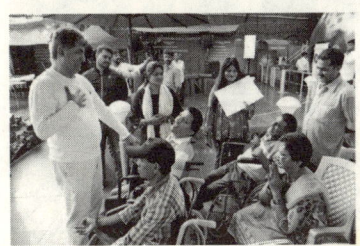
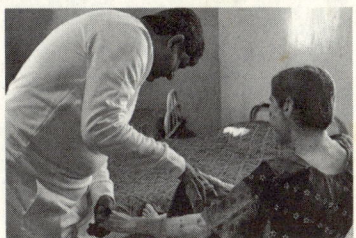

HAPPINESS IS SUCCESS

AiR WITH HIS FAMILY OF 700. SHIVA WAS BROUGHT TO AiR HUMANITARIAN HOMES 25 YEARS AGO.

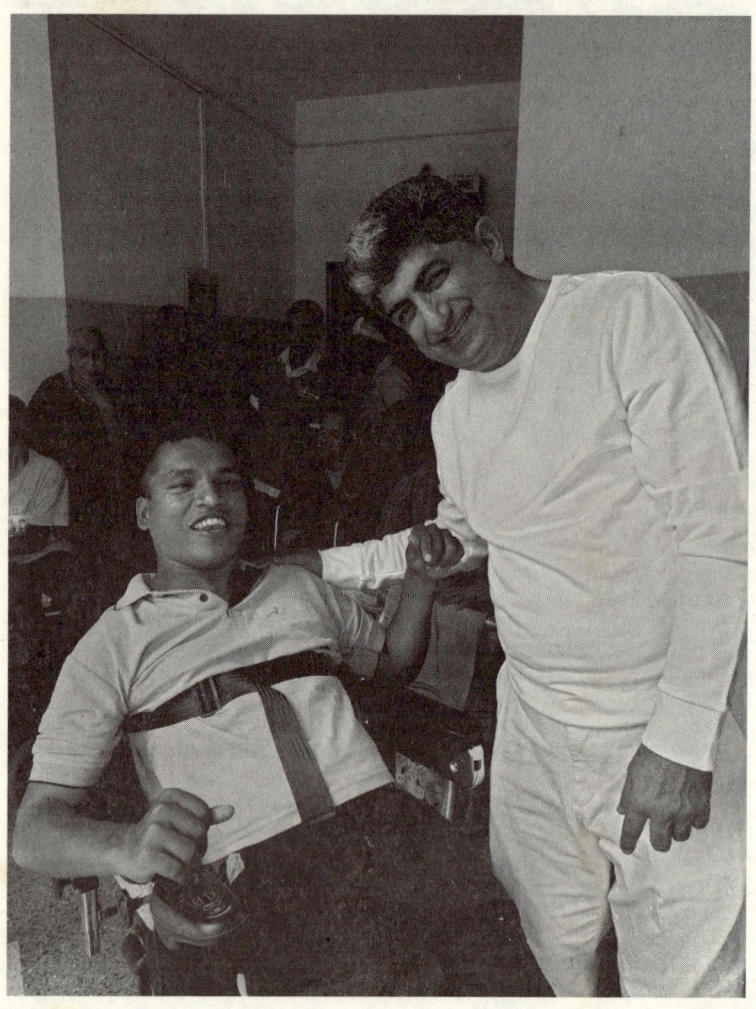

LIST OF BOOKS BY AiR

1. Talaash
2. 3 Peaks of Happiness
3. My Guru, My Mentor, My God on Earth
4. I will Never Die. Death is not 'The End'
5. Death is Not 'The End'. Death is 'Liberation'
6. I am not I. Who am I?
7. The Mind is a Rascal
8. A Cosmic Drama
9. Who is God? Where is God? What is God?
10. The A to Z of Karma
11. Who Are You & Why Are You Here?
12. The 4th Factor
13. Be Happy in the NOW!
14. Questions You Must Answer Before You Die
15. Suffer No More
16. Success is not Happiness, Happiness is Success
17. God = Happiness
18. Life! Realized!!
19. True Love is Bliss, Not Just a Kiss
20. True Meaning of Yoga
21. The Ultimate Goal of Life, MEN – Moksha, Enlightenment, Nirvana
22. Religion! A Kindergarten to Spirituality
23. Why Bad-things can't Happen to Good people
24. LIFE is – Liberation from Ignorance and Finding true Enlightenment

25. The Ladder to Heaven
26. FEAR – False Expectations Appearing Real
27. Soul – We don't have a Soul, We are the Soul!
28. But we Pray
29. EGOD – Let Go of your Ego and you will find God
30. 100 Diamond Quotes
31. Life Manual
32. Peace
33. SatChitAnanda
34. Neti Neti Tat Twam Asi
35. The Law of AttrACTION
36. Satyam Shivam Sundaram
37. My Enlightenment Lifebook
38. When you overcome the Fear of Death, You start to Live
39. World Peace! A Simple Solution
40. Many Problems, One Solution
41. LIVE LIFE, Moment by Moment
42. The Spiritual Jigsaw Puzzle
43. The 4 Quarters of Life
44. Rebirth
45. How to Live a Spiritual Life in a Material World?
46. Life is Karma
47. Poems for Life – Peace, Love, Bliss, Enlightenment and Eternal Happiness
48. Enlightenment – The Myth and The Truth
49. God is not God, God is SIP
50. The 10 Commands of Detached Attachment
51. Prema Yoga – The Yoga of Divine Love
52. Give, Before you are Gone!
53. Mukti-Freedom
54. Stop it, Stupid! Discover the Mantra of Happiness
55. Don't cut your cake! Awake! Your birthday is Fake
56. Realizations of a Yogi
57. Flip over from Mind to Consciousness